W9-BEY-737

Hate Groups

TAMARA L. ROLEFF

OPPOSING
VIEWPOINTS®
DIGESTS

Greenhaven Press, Inc., San Diego, California

No part of this book may be reproduced or used in any form or by any means, electrical, mechanical, or otherwise, including, but not limited to, photocopy, recording, or any information storage and retrieval system, without prior written permission from the publisher.

Every effort has been made to trace owners of copyrighted material.

Library of Congress Cataloging-in-Publication Data

Roleff, Tamara L., 1959–
  Hate groups / by Tamara L. Roleff.
    p. cm. — (Opposing viewpoints digests)
  Includes bibliographical references and index.
  ISBN 0-7377-0677-5 (hardback : alk. paper) — ISBN 0-7377-0676-7
  (pbk. : alk. paper)
  1. Hate crimes—United States—Juvenile literature. 2. Hate groups—
United States—Juvenile literature. [1. Hate crimes. 2. Hate groups.
3. White supremacy movements.] I. Title. II. Series.

HV6773.52 .H369 2001
364.1—dc21
                                                    00-012170

Cover Photo: © Steve Liss/The Liaison Agency Network
©AFP/Corbis: 29
Library of Congress: 7, 9
©Adam Mastoon/Corbis: 71
Reuters/Jim Bourg/Archive Photos: 37
©Reuters NewMedia Inc./Corbis: 13, 20, 63

©2001 by Greenhaven Press, Inc.
PO Box 289009, San Diego, CA 92198-9009

Printed in the U.S.A.

CONTENTS

FOREWORD

The only way in which a human being can make some approach to knowing the whole of a subject is by hearing what can be said about it by persons of every variety of opinion and studying all modes in which it can be looked at by every character of mind. No wise man ever acquired his wisdom in any mode but this.

—John Stuart Mill

Today, young adults are inundated with a wide variety of points of view on an equally wide spectrum of subjects. Often overshadowing traditional books and newspapers as forums for these views are a host of broadcast, print, and electronic media, including television news and entertainment programs, talk shows, and commercials; radio talk shows and call-in lines; movies, home videos, and compact discs; magazines and supermarket tabloids; and the increasingly popular and influential Internet.

For teenagers, this multiplicity of sources, ideas, and opinions can be both positive and negative. On the one hand, a wealth of useful, interesting, and enlightening information is readily available virtually at their fingertips, underscoring the need for teens to recognize and consider a wide range of views besides their own. As Mark Twain put it, "It were not best that we should all think alike; it is difference of opinion that makes horse races." On the other hand, the range of opinions on a given subject is often too wide to absorb and analyze easily. Trying to keep up with, sort out, and form personal opinions from such a barrage can be daunting for anyone, let alone young people who have not yet acquired effective critical judgment skills.

Moreover, to the task of evaluating this assortment of impersonal information, many teenagers bring firsthand experience of serious and emotionally charged social and health problems, including divorce, family violence, alcoholism and drug abuse, rape, unwanted pregnancy, the spread of AIDS, and eating disorders. Teens are often forced to deal with these problems before they are capable of objective opinion based on reason and judgment. All too often, teens' response to these deep personal issues is impulsive rather than carefully considered.

Greenhaven Press's Opposing Viewpoints Digests are designed to aid in examining important current issues in a way that develops critical thinking and evaluating skills. Each book presents thought-provoking argument and stimulating debate on a single issue. By examining an issue from many different points of view, readers come to realize its complexity and acknowledge the validity of opposing opinions. This insight is especially helpful in writing reports, research papers, and persuasive essays, when students must competently address common objections and controversies related to their topic. In addition, examination of the diverse mix of opinions in each volume challenges readers to question their own strongly held opinions and assumptions. While the point of such examination is not to change readers' minds, examining views that oppose their own will certainly deepen their own knowledge of the issue and help them realize exactly why they hold the opinion they do.

The Opposing Viewpoints Digests offer a number of unique features that sharpen young readers' critical thinking and reading skills. To assure an appropriate and consistent reading level for young adults, all essays in each volume are written by a single author. Each essay heavily quotes readable primary sources that are fully cited to allow for further research and documentation. Thus, primary sources are introduced in a context to enhance comprehension.

In addition, each volume includes extensive research tools. A section containing relevant source material includes interviews, excerpts from original research, and the opinions of prominent spokespersons. A "facts about" section allows students to peruse relevant facts and statistics; these statistics are also fully cited, allowing students to question and analyze the credibility of the source. Two bibliographies, one for young adults and one listing the author's sources, are also included; both are annotated to guide student research. Finally, a comprehensive index allows students to scan and locate content efficiently.

Greenhaven's Opposing Viewpoints Digests, like Greenhaven's higher level and critically acclaimed Opposing Viewpoints Series, have been developed around the concept that an awareness and appreciation for the complexity of seemingly simple issues is particularly important in a democratic society. In a democracy, the common good is often, and very appropriately, decided by open debate of widely varying views. As one of our democracy's greatest advocates, Thomas Jefferson, observed, "Difference of opinion leads to inquiry, and inquiry to truth." It is to this principle that Opposing Viewpoints Digests are dedicated.

An Overview of Hate Groups and the Attempts to Fight Them

The U.S. government has been fighting hate groups since the founding of the Ku Klux Klan after the Civil War. The Klan, also known as the KKK, is one of the most notorious hate groups in history. It was formed on Christmas Eve 1865 in Pulaski, Tennessee, by six bored veterans of the Confederate army. The men named their club after the Greek word for circle, *kuklos*, and added "Klan" because they were all of Scottish or Irish descent. The group's original purpose was "purely social and for our amusement,"[1] according to one of its founders, James Crowe. It started innocently enough with harmless pranks such as gate-crashing private parties. Then one night the KKK members dressed themselves and their horses in sheets and marched through town. They were delighted by the response to their parade—mystified and shocked comments by the white townsfolk, and reports of fear from the recently freed black slaves.

KKK History

Membership in the secretive KKK organization spread rapidly, with chapters springing up not only elsewhere in Tennessee but also in Mississippi and Alabama. The first national convention was held in Nashville in 1867. During the convention, the KKK decided the South needed an "organization capable of defending her rights"[2] against the Reconstructionists—northerners who had taken control of state and local governments after the war. Another of the organization's goals was to maintain "the supremacy of the White Race in this Republic."[3] Angry, defeated southerners resented attempts by freed black slaves to upset what they regarded as the natural balance of white superiority and black subordination. They were alarmed by what they considered the insolence of previously docile

An illustration from an 1868 newspaper shows two Ku Klux Klan members in their hoods and robes.

black slaves toward their former white masters: Blacks were mixing freely with whites in public, greeting white women on the street, and refusing to work for their former masters for free. White southerners, who were vastly outnumbered by blacks, also feared losing political power and control to former slaves who now had the power of the vote. To put blacks back in their place and to strike out at the northerners who were forcing fundamental change on southern culture, Klan members began harassing, terrorizing, torturing, and frequently murdering black freedmen and their white supporters.

Eventually the Klan's national leader, Nathan Forrest, realized that he was no longer able to control the Klan's members, who now routinely murdered and lynched anyone—white or black—who annoyed them for the most trivial reasons. In 1869, Forrest officially dissolved the organization—which had grown to an estimated 550,000 members—in part because he believed it was no longer a "protective, political, military organization,"[4] and in part because he feared a congressional investigation into Ku Klux Klan activities.

The First Attempts to Control Hate

Congress had decided to investigate the Klan in response to many complaints about the abuses, threats, and violence suffered by blacks and white Reconstructionists. Its first action was to pass the Civil Rights Act of 1866, which overturned many southern state laws that prohibited blacks from making contracts, filing suit, giving evidence in court, and owning property. The act also decreed that blacks were entitled to equal protection under the law. In 1866, when Congress realized that the South was still ignoring black rights, it passed the Fourteenth Amendment, which made equality under the law a part of the Constitution when it was ratified by the states in 1868. In 1870 the states ratified the Fifteenth Amendment, which gave all blacks—not just emancipated slaves—the right to vote.

Congress then passed the Ku Klux Klan Act in 1871, allowing U.S. citizens to sue, in federal court, anyone who deprived them of their constitutionally protected rights. The act also

Members of the Ku Klux Klan march down Pennsylvania Avenue in Washington, D.C., in 1925.

created a new crime: conspiracy to deprive a person of his civil rights. It was now illegal for two or more people to "conspire together, or go in disguise upon the public highway or upon the premises of another"[5] to prevent him from exercising any of his constitutionally protected rights. The act also gave the president the authority to use military force to subdue protests or riots that threatened a citizen's rights.

According to Wyn Craig Wade, author of *The Fiery Cross: The Ku Klux Klan in America*, the Klan's activities actually helped American blacks attain their constitutional rights. He writes, "So long as an organized, secret conspiracy swore oaths and used cloak-and-dagger methods in the South, Congress was willing to legislate against it—legislation that would provide vital safeguards for the cause of racial equality in the future."[6]

The Ku Klux Klan's Second Era

Following the government crackdown in the 1870s, the Klan disappeared for a few decades. It reemerged in 1915 following the release of the silent film *Birth of a Nation*, which portrayed the KKK as the savior of the South's way of life during Reconstruction. William Simmons was inspired by the film to revive the organization, and he is responsible for bringing the Klan out of the deep South and into the North and heartland of America. Under Simmons, the Klan extended its antiblack bias to Jews, Asians, immigrants, and Catholics. In the early 1920s, an estimated 4 million people belonged to the Ku Klux Klan, including Warren G. Harding, the president of the United States, and Hugo Black, a Supreme Court justice. However, after several scandals involving high-ranking Klan leaders, membership plummeted to about forty thousand by 1930. The organization officially disbanded for a second time in 1944 when the federal government presented it with a bill of $685,000 for back taxes on its earnings during the 1920s.

The Klan rallied again during the 1950s following the landmark Supreme Court decision that overturned the practice of "separate but equal" racial segregation in *Brown v. Board of Education*. The Court ruled that this policy of segregation—in which the races had not only separate schools, but also eating areas in restaurants, bus and train waiting areas, pools, and even drinking fountains—was unconstitutional. It ordered that schools must be desegregated, an action many southerners and the KKK opposed. During the next two decades, the KKK fought against black equality with terrorism, torture, bombings, murders and lynchings, and other horrific crimes of violence. Often disguised in their trademark hoods and white robes, Klan members were rarely arrested for their crimes against blacks; those who were usually were acquitted by all-white juries. In an ironic abuse of justice, the black victims were usually found guilty of some crimes, such as assaulting their white attackers.

Typical of many southerners' feelings toward blacks are these comments by Matt Murphy Jr., an attorney who defended three Klansmen who shot and killed a white woman who was driving blacks to a march in Selma, Alabama, in 1965:

I'm proud to be a white man and I'm proud that I stand up on my feet for white supremacy. Not black supremacy, not the mixing and mongrelization of the races. . . . Integration breaks every moral law God ever wrote. Noah's son was Ham and committed adultery and was banished and his sons were Hamites and God banished them and they went to Africa and the only thing they ever built was grass huts. No white woman can ever marry a descendant of Ham. That's God's law. . . . I don't care what [President] Lyndon Johnson or anybody else says.[7]

Despite the fact that the defendants killed the woman in front of witnesses, including an FBI agent who had infiltrated the group, the Klansmen were acquitted.

Finally, by the 1960s, many Americans began to condemn Klan violence in connection with the development of the modern civil rights movement. States passed laws against the Klan, such as statutes prohibiting the wearing of masks in public. In response to protests and sit-ins against Jim Crow laws (which authorized segregation and discrimination), cities passed laws permitting desegregation in all areas of public life. Congress passed the Civil Rights Acts of 1964 and 1968 (the first major civil rights legislation since 1875), which guaranteed constitutional rights in public places and prohibited discrimination based on race, color, religion, sex, or national origin in education and federal programs. It also passed the Voting Rights Act of 1965, which outlawed literacy tests for blacks and other impediments to voting. As a result, Klan membership declined steadily. In 1974, Klan membership was estimated to have fallen to an all-time low of fifteen hundred.

Hate Groups Today

In the 1980s, several Klan members left the KKK and started their own white supremacy organizations. One of the first to leave was Tom Metzger, who founded the White American Political Association in California, which he renamed White

Aryan Resistance (WAR) in 1984. As the acronym suggests, WAR is a more militant organization than most other white supremacist groups. Metzger chose the name deliberately, he said, to show he was serious about the group's goals: "It was an ideological change. And I liked the acronym: WAR. When you choose words, it is very important to choose strong ones. WAR was a deliberate move to scare off the weak-kneed people from my group. It worked."[8]

Another offshoot of the Klan is the Church of Jesus Christ Christian-Aryan Nations, or simply Aryan Nations. The organization believes that only members of the white race are the true descendants of the biblical Adam. Since the late 1980s, hundreds, if not thousands of other white supremacist groups have appeared.

New ways of fighting hate have been developed with the emergence of new hate groups and white supremacist and white separatist organizations. During the 1980s, many colleges, workplaces, and cities instituted regulations banning hate speech, which is generally defined as speech that demeans or degrades a person or a group. Supporters of speech codes believe that hate speech directed at minorities and women silences them and prevents them from participating fully in society. However, opponents contend that speech codes violate the right to free speech, and the Supreme Court has tended to agree, ruling that many speech codes are unconstitutional.

Cities and states also fight hate groups through hate crime laws. Such laws maintain that certain groups, such as racial, ethnic, and religious minorities, women, and sometimes homosexuals and the disabled, have historically been subject to persecution and discrimination. The laws impose extra penalties on convicted offenders whose crime victim was chosen solely because he or she belongs to a protected group. Supporters of hate crime laws claim that they are needed to show that society will not tolerate crimes committed on the basis of bigotry and intolerance. Opponents contend that hate crime laws violate the Fourteenth Amendment, which guarantees all citizens equality under the law. They argue that hate crime laws treat a criminal convicted of a hate crime more severely than a criminal convicted of an identical crime not based on hate. That, opponents assert, creates two classes of criminals and is therefore unconstitutional.

Civil Lawsuits Against Hate Groups

A tactic that is being used more frequently to fight hate and hate groups is to sue the organization with which a criminal is affiliated for violating the victim's civil rights. Morris Dees of the Southern Poverty Law Center has used this strategy several times quite successfully. In 1981 the SPLC won an injunction against the Ku Klux Klan in Texas for harassing and intimidating Vietnamese shrimp fishermen. It also won a $12.5 million fine in 1990 against WAR founder Metzger and his son John Metzger for the unlawful death of an Ethiopian immigrant, Mulugeta Seraw, in Portland, Oregon. Dees convinced a

The Southern Poverty Law Center won a $12.5 million fine against Tom Metzger (pictured), founder of White Aryan Resistance.

Portland jury that the Metzgers were responsible for Seraw's murder because they had direct links to the skinheads who murdered him. In 1998, the SPLC won its largest award ever: The Christian Knights of the Ku Klux Klan and its leader, Horace King, were ordered to pay a $37.8 million fine for burning a black Baptist church in South Carolina in 1995.

Most recently, Dees and the center won a $6.3 million verdict against the Aryan Nations in September 2000. The case—while not a hate crime—involved three members of the Aryan Nations who, while guarding the entrance to their compound in Hayden Lake, Idaho, chased, shot at, and assaulted Victoria Keenan and her son Jason when the guards mistook a backfire from the Keenans' car for gunshots. The guards were subsequently convicted of aggravated assault. The Keenans, along with Dees and the SPLC, followed up the criminal trial with a civil suit for punitive damages against the guards and Richard Butler, leader of the Aryan Nations. Dees maintains that Butler was negligent in hiring, training, and supervising his guards because one was emotionally unstable, one had previously been charged with assault, and none had received any security training.

Although Butler admitted that he is the leader of the Aryan Nations, he testified during his trial that he is not liable for the actions of his security guards. "I have no power of command. We're a volunteer organization. Sometimes, all you can do is guide them in what you are trying to do."[9] Butler's lawyer, Edgar Steele, argued that the Keenans' lawsuit really meant to punish his ideas, not the assault. Steele maintained that Butler's beliefs—hateful as they are—should not be on trial. He warned that a victory for Dees and the Keenans would be a strike against the First Amendment's right to free speech. "I'm not really defending Richard Butler," Steele maintained. "I'm defending all of our rights to say something unpopular. . . . The battle for the First Amendment is never pretty. And it always involves very unattractive defendants, because those are the only people that the establishment wants to shut up."[10]

After less than two days of deliberation, the jury awarded the Keenans $6.3 million in compensatory and punitive damages from Butler, the security guards, and Aryan Nations. Dees says he intends to force Butler to surrender the Aryan Nations compound and every other asset of the group, including the name. "This judgment bankrupts Butler, but he was bankrupt from the start because his ideas are corrupt and evil,"[11] Dees asserts.

Still Operational

Metzger contends that even though his and other white supremacy groups have been bankrupted by lawsuits, the organizations are still operational. In fact, he adds, driving these groups out of business may work against hate-monitoring groups such as the Southern Poverty Law Center because the white supremacist organizations will go underground rather than give up their beliefs. And once they're underground, he maintains, they will be much more difficult to track. "I lost my little old house, a small business, and my wife," Metzger says, but "I never stopped publishing my newspaper."[12]

The editors of the *Washington Post* also believe that the lawsuit and judgment against the Aryan Nations may be misguided. Only $300,000 of the award is designated as compensation; the remaining $6 million represents punitive damages. The two purposes of such a large award are 1) to bankrupt the organization so it is much less capable of harming individuals and society and 2) to send a message that hate will not be tolerated. Although the editors agree that these goals are admirable, they warn that it is dangerous to award damages "based on who the defendants are, rather than for the specific wrongful acts they commit."[13] They caution society to carefully consider lawsuits whose sole purpose is to bankrupt an organization with unpopular beliefs, as views on what speech should be considered hateful, and therefore suppressed, can easily change.

Changing Attitudes

Lawsuits against hate groups have thus sparked the same controversies that surround hate crime laws and codes against hate speech. While few people defend hate as a concept, many are uncomfortable with the idea of making hate illegal. On the other hand, opponents of hate groups argue that while individuals are entitled to hold racist or hateful *views*, organized hate groups encourage individuals to *act* on those beliefs, which is illegal.

Messages of hate, fear, and intimidation have been fought as long as hate groups have been in existence. Many people believe that legislation—and in the Keenans' case, litigation—will do little to suppress hate. Others argue that legislation is needed to show hate groups that their actions are unacceptable. At any rate, legislation and education are often the first steps toward changing attitudes. Whether they will be effective is yet to be seen.

1. Quoted in Paul Elliott, *Brotherhoods of Fear: A History of Violent Organizations*. New York: Sterling, 1998, p. 53.

2. Elliott, *Brotherhoods of Fear*, p. 56.

3. Quoted in Betty A. Dobratz and Stephanie L. Shanks-Meile, *"White Power, White Pride!" The White Separatist Movement in the United States*. New York: Twayne, 1997, p. 36.

4. Elliott, *Brotherhoods of Fear*, p. 56.

5. Quoted in David M. Chalmers, *Hooded Americanism: The History of the Ku Klux Klan*. Durham, NC: Duke University Press, 1998, p. 90.

6. Wyn Craig Wade, *The Fiery Cross: The Ku Klux Klan in America*. New York: Oxford University Press, 1987, p. 111.

7. Quoted in Richard K. Tucker, *The Dragon and the Cross: The Rise and Fall of the Ku Klux Klan in Middle America*. Hamden, CT: Archon Books, 1991, pp. 189–90.

8. Quoted in Dobratz and Shanks-Meile, *"White Power, White Pride!"* p. 50.

9. Quoted in Mike McLean, "Judge Says Butler Can Be Held Liable for Guards' Assault," *Coeur d'Alene Press Online*, September 2, 2000, www.cdapress.com/archives/0902/news2.html.

10. Quoted in Mike McLean, "Edgar Steele Speaks Out," *Coeur d'Alene Press Online*, September 5, 2000, www.cdapress.com/archives/0905/news2.html.

11. Quoted in Mike McLean, "Aryans Lose," *Coeur d'Alene Press Online*, September 8, 2000, www.cdapress.com/archives/0908/news2.html.

12. Quoted in Mike McLean, "Litigation Pushing Racists Underground," *Coeur d'Alene Press Online*, September 6, 2000, www.cdapress.com/archives/0906/news2.html.

13. *Washington Post*, "The Aryan Nations Verdict," September 16, 2000, p. A18.

CHAPTER 1

Are Hate Groups a Serious Problem?

"The decline in the numbers of organized hate groups . . . is misleading, because membership in the largest groups is increasing at astounding rates."

Hate Groups Are a Serious Problem

There is no building, no altar, and no god to worship in the World Church of the Creator, based in East Peoria, Illinois. The pastor of this "church," twenty-eight-year-old Matthew Hale, preaches not love and forgiveness of his fellow man, but rather hate and violence toward anyone who is not white. In the summer of 1999, one of the "church's" followers acted on that creed. Benjamin N. Smith, who changed his name to "August" because Benjamin sounded too Jewish, went on a three-day shooting rampage in Illinois and Indiana.

On Friday, July 2, Smith wounded six Orthodox Jews in Chicago who were leaving their synagogue after worshiping on the Jewish Sabbath. Smith then drove to Skokie, Illinois, where he shot and killed Ricky Byrdsong, the forty-three-year-old black former basketball coach at Northwestern University, as he was walking with his children down the street. From Skokie, Smith then drove to the suburb of Northbrook, Illinois, where he fired at an Asian couple.

On Saturday, July 3, Smith fired on two black men in Springfield, Illinois. Later that same day, Smith fired into a group of Asian men standing on a corner near the University of Illinois in Champaign-Urbana, hitting a graduate student in the leg. The next day, Sunday, July 4, Smith sat in his light blue Ford Taurus outside a Korean United Methodist Church in Bloomington, Indiana. As the church service let out, Smith fired four shots into a group of Korean worshipers. Won-Joon Yoon, a twenty-six-year-old student at the University of Indiana, was shot twice in the back of the head and killed. Smith fled, then abandoned his car at a truck stop in Salem, Illinois, and carjacked a van. During a high-speed police chase, Smith shot and killed himself.

Too Much Hatred

Though this terrorist is dead, the residents of Bloomington, Indiana, and surrounding areas do not feel any safer. "Ben Smith may have taken his own life, but there's still far too much hatred out there, in the community, in the world," maintains Sue Shifron, a rabbi who founded Bloomington United, an organization that was formed in response to racist leaflets Smith was distributing in the city. "While he may be gone, the organization that he was a part of and hundreds of other organizations are still out there."[1]

Indeed, a study by the hate-monitoring group Center for New Community found that one year after Smith's shooting rampage, the World Church of the Creator "remains a magnet for young, volatile white supremacists."[2] According to the CNC, membership in the "church" has nearly doubled. Although Hale refuses to divulge the number of dues-paying members in his group, the center says WCOTC has added thirty-five chapters since Smith's hate crime spree, for a total of seventy-six, an increase of 85 percent. And, the center adds, Hale's organization is attracting female as well as male white supremacists; two women's groups—the Sisterhood of the WCOTC and Women's Frontier—have both grown, from three to six chapters and from two to four chapters, respectively.

The World Church of the Creator is not alone in its growth spurt. Other hate groups are also adding to their membership rolls. The Southern Poverty Law Center, preeminent among organizations that monitor hate groups, reports that the decline

The number of chapters in the World Church of the Creator, led by Matthew Hale (far right), has increased an estimated 85 percent since 1999.

in the numbers of organized hate groups across the United States during the latter half of the 1990s is misleading, because membership in the largest groups is increasing at astounding rates. Larger organizations, the SPLC explains, are absorbing the members of many of the smaller hate groups that are folding. According to Joseph T. Roy, director of the SPLC's *Intelligence Report*, "The situation's deeply worrying. Many of the less active and isolated smaller groups have joined forces with much more serious players. There is strong evidence that far more people are now in really hard-line groups like the National Alliance and Hammerskin Nation."[3] Hammerskin Nation, the world's largest coalition of neo-Nazi skinheads, increased the number of its chapters by 70 percent in 1999. And although the National Alliance actually lost three chapters in 1999, its total membership has doubled since 1992.

The National Alliance

The National Alliance is of particular concern to the Anti-Defamation League, an organization that monitors anti-Semitism, bigotry, and hate crimes. The ADL reports that the National Alliance, a neo-Nazi group also active in Europe, "is the single most dangerous organized hate group in the United States today."[4] It contends that members of the National Alliance are responsible for dozens of violent hate crimes across the country, including murders, bombings, and robberies.

The ADL credits the growth of the National Alliance to several factors: vigorous recruitment drives, especially in innocuous settings, such as gun shows; innovative promotional activities, such as a "European-American Cultural Fest" held in Cleveland in 1998; cooperation with other hate groups, especially violent skinhead groups; and its use of technology, such as the Internet, to spread its vicious propaganda.

The Internet

Many hate-monitoring groups are especially concerned about how hate groups such as World Church of the Creator and

National Alliance use the Internet to spread their message. The first known hate site on the Internet was Stormfront, established in 1995 by Don Black, a former member of the Ku Klux Klan. By early 2000, organized hate groups maintained more than three hundred hate sites, and as many as two thousand hate sites were unaffiliated with any group. Black explains why the Internet is such an important tool for hate groups: "The Net has changed everything. We suddenly have a mass audience rather than a small clique of subscribers."[5]

Before the advent of the Internet, hate groups "needed to put out substantial effort and money to produce and distribute a shoddy pamphlet that might reach one hundred people," notes Roy. "Today, with a $500 computer and negligible other costs, [hate groups] can put up a slickly produced Web site with a potential audience in the millions." And the audience the hate groups are targeting is the one most likely to be at their computers surfing the Web: affluent, college-bound teenagers who could be the movement's future leaders. As Roy puts it, these "middle- and upper-middle-class youths . . . wouldn't be caught dead at a Klan rally," but in the privacy of their bedroom they are much more willing to talk about racist or anti-Semitic beliefs. However, as Roy points out, "There is no real exchange of ideas on www.whitepower.com."[6]

The Internet has proved to be a bonanza to hate groups. Hate groups are able to reach potential recruits at younger and younger ages, which could result in "much younger, more committed bigots than we've ever seen before in our nation,"[7] according to Abraham Cooper, a rabbi with the Simon Wiesenthal Center in Los Angeles. The destructive potential that hate groups have gained through their websites is horrifying to contemplate.

1. Quoted in Bill Dedman, "Midwest Gunman Had Engaged in Racist Acts at Two Universities," *New York Times*, July 6, 1999, p. A1.

2. Center for New Community, "World Church of the Creator: One Year Later," June 26, 2000, www.newcomm.org/bdi/wcotc.pdf.

3. Quoted in Southern Poverty Law Center, "The Year in Hate," *Intelligence Report*, Winter 2000, www.splcenter.org/intelligenceproject/ip-4m2.html.

4. Anti-Defamation League, "Explosion of Hate: The Growing Danger of the National Alliance," www.adl.org/explosion_of_hate/explosion_of_hate.html.

5. Quoted in Jared Sandberg, "Spinning a Web of Hate," *Newsweek*, July 19, 1999, p. 28.

6. Joseph T. Roy, testimony before the U.S. Senate Committee on the Judiciary, "Hate on the Internet," September 14, 1999.

7. Quoted in Sandberg, "Spinning a Web of Hate," p. 28.

"Few hate crimes are committed by hate groups."

Hate Groups Are Not a Serious Problem

White supremacist groups such as the Ku Klux Klan, World Church of the Creator, and Aryan Nations have become more familiar to many Americans in the past few years due to a few highly publicized attacks by the groups' members against minorities. In June 1998, John William King, who had ties to the KKK, and two other men killed James Byrd Jr. in Jasper, Texas, by dragging him to pieces behind King's pickup. Just over a year later, Benjamin Smith, a member of the World Church of the Creator, went on a shooting spree of minorities in Indiana and Illinois, killing two people and wounding nine others in early July 1999. In August 1999, Buford O. Furrow, an avowed racist affiliated with Aryan Nations, shot four children and a receptionist at a Jewish community center in Los Angeles before killing a Filipino mail carrier, Joseph Ileto.

These hate crimes—deplorable as they are—are not an indication that America has declared war on minorities. Most Americans do not consider themselves racist and reject white supremacists' prejudice against minorities. Consequently, hate groups are having little success enlisting new members to their cause. As the organizations fail to reach their recruiting and fundraising goals, frustration among the groups' white supremacist members rises and they elect to use more and more dramatic means of calling attention to themselves and their points of view.

According to David A. Lehrer, regional director of the Anti-Defamation League (ADL) of B'nai B'rith in Los Angeles, these hate crimes "are acts of violent desperation on the part of those who are not succeeding in swaying the world to their views." These incidents, he adds, are "a perverted and desperate effort to attract media and public attention"[1] to the cause of bigotry.

Declining Numbers

Perhaps because white supremacist organizations are having difficulty recruiting new members, the number of hate groups has declined. The Southern Poverty Law Center (SPLC), an organization that closely monitors white supremacists, militias, and antigovernment and other hate groups, counted 457 hate groups in 1999, down from a high of 858 in 1996. Several organizations, including the National Alliance, a neo-Nazi group, and Christian Identity, an organization based on anti-Semitic theology, have reported that they have lost chapters or canceled annual conferences due to a lack of interest among their members. The SPLC theorizes that the reason for the decline in the number of active organizations may be that the "weekend warriors" who once made up the groups' ranks "have gone home, tired of waiting for a revolution that never comes and turned off by the violence the movement produces."[2] Tom Metzger, leader of the neo-Nazi group White Aryan Resistance, based in Fallbrook, California, agrees: "All membership organizations are [currently] either treading water or losing ground. . . . Many [members] will turn informant, rationalizing that we barbarians have just gone too far."[3]

The decrease in the number of hate groups during the late 1990s was accompanied by a steady decline in the number of hate crimes reported to the FBI. In 1998, the federal agency received 7,775 reports of hate crimes, compared with 8,049 in 1997 and a high of 8,759 in 1996. According to FBI statistics, most hate crimes are nonviolent: intimidation was the single most frequently reported hate crime (about 39 percent), followed by vandalism (26 percent to 28 percent).

Studies of hate crimes reveal that hate groups are responsible for very few of the attacks reported to the FBI. According to Jack Levin and Jack McDevitt, coauthors of *Hate Crimes: The Rising Tide of Bigotry and Bloodshed*, the majority of hate crimes—about two-thirds—are committed by "thrill seekers," who are usually "bored and alienated youngsters looking for excitement in bashing or assaulting someone who is different."[4] Levin and McDevitt term the second-largest category of hate crimes (about one-third) "defensive" because the perpetrators feel "personally threatened" by the presence of minorities who have moved into environments that have previously been all-white, such as neighborhoods or schools. Finally, they note, fewer than 1 percent of hate crimes are committed by what analysts call "true believers"—those members of organized hate groups who are motivated by white-supremacist philosophy and believe it is their "mission" to eliminate people of a despised race.

Lone Wolves

The FBI, other law enforcement agencies, and researchers also confirm Levin and McDevitt's conclusion that few hate crimes are committed by hate groups. They have found that up to 95 percent

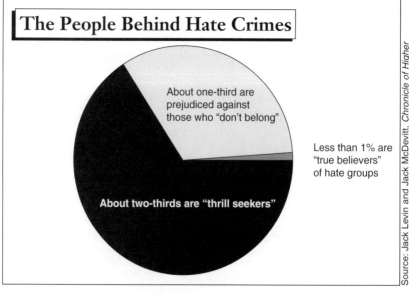

The People Behind Hate Crimes

About one-third are prejudiced against those who "don't belong"

Less than 1% are "true believers" of hate groups

About two-thirds are "thrill seekers"

Source: Jack Levin and Jack McDevitt, *Chronicle of Higher Education*, August 4, 1995.

of all hate crimes are committed by individuals—known as "lone wolves"—who act independently and are not part of a conspiracy by hate groups to attack specific targets. "We've moved into the era of the solo act,"[5] maintains Mike Reynolds, an analyst at the SPLC. These lone wolves are conducting their own private wars against minorities, homosexuals, and the government. According to Brian Jenkins, a crime and terrorism analyst at the Rand Corporation, a research organization, "We've moved into a realm where . . . individuals . . . mentally incorporate the belief systems, whether it's racism or anti-Semitism or religious fanaticism, of the broader universe, but are not receiving orders in any formal sense of the term."[6] However, Levin, McDevitt, Jenkins, and others who study hate crimes maintain that lone wolves are even more dangerous than hate groups because the individuals have few tangible links to hate groups, cannot be infiltrated by the FBI, and are nearly impossible to identify in advance of their attacks.

The murders by King, Smith, and Furrow demonstrate the danger posed by individuals and how difficult it is for law enforcement to detect and prevent such horrible crimes. Despite the fact that the men were or had been members of various white supremacist groups at one time, they alone are responsible for their horrible crimes. These men all acted on their own initiative, not on orders from a group. It is not organized hate groups that America should worry about, but individual white men acting on their own anger.

1. David Lehrer, "Tolerance, Not Hate, Is on the Rise," *Los Angeles Times*, August 13, 1999, p. B7.

2. Southern Poverty Law Center, "Fewer, but Harder," www.splcenter.org/teachingtolerance/tt-index.html.

3. Quoted in Southern Poverty Law Center, "The Year in Hate," *Intelligence Report*, Winter 2000, www.splcenter.org/intelligenceproject/ip-4m2.html.

4. Jack Levin and Jack McDevitt, "The Research Needed to Understand Hate Crime," *Chronicle of Higher Education*, August 4, 1995, p. B1.

5. Quoted in Jo Thomas, "New Face of Terror Crimes: 'Lone Wolf' Weaned on Hate," *New York Times*, August 16, 1999, p. A1.

6. Quoted in Thomas, "New Face of Terror Crimes," p. A1.

"Racist hate groups and their members are dangerous. They are an immense threat to America's peace and security."

Racist Groups Promote Hate and Violence

One morning in August 1999, on a quiet tree-lined street in a Los Angeles suburb, Buford Furrow walked into the North Valley Jewish Community Center with a high-powered rifle and started shooting. Isabelle Shalometh, the center's sixty-eight-year-old receptionist, was his first victim, shot in the arm as she ducked behind her desk. Mindy Finkelstein, a sixteen-year-old youth counselor, was shot in the back and arm as she tried to flee. A five-year-old boy was the most critically wounded, shot in the stomach. And Furrow shot two six-year-old boys, one in the foot, the other in the leg and hip. After spraying more than seventy bullets in the building's lobby and halls, Furrow left the center, abandoned his van—which contained several handguns, an assault rifle, and thousands of rounds of ammunition—at a suburban airport, and hijacked a car. Within an hour of the shooting at the Jewish community center, Furrow gunned down Joseph Ileto, a thirty-nine-year-old Filipino-American postal carrier, with nine bullets from a Glock handgun, leaving him to die in a driveway on his mail route.

Some say that Furrow shot innocent children at the Jewish community center and killed a Filipino postal worker because

he was crazy, and they may have a point: Furrow was hospital-
ized for mental illness for a month a year earlier. However, it
wasn't mental illness that made him choose Jews and a Filipino
for his targets; it was the extremist, hate-filled ideology he
learned while he was a follower of the virulently racist hate
groups Aryan Nations and Christian Identity. Furrow learned
and was encouraged to hate minorities as an adherent of these
white supremacist organizations.

White Supremacist Beliefs

The theology of many white supremacist groups holds that
Jews and minorities are subhuman, the descendants of Eve and
Satan—who seduced her—or "beasts," who were created by
God before Adam and Eve. According to the white supremacist
World Church of the Creator, the white race has "risen to the
very top of the human scale," while there are "varying gradua-
tions of subhuman species below." The black race, it adds, is "at

*Buford Furrow (pictured) went on a rampage in 1999, shooting at people in a
Jewish community center and later killing a postal worker.*

the very bottom of the ladder, not far above monkeys and chimpanzees."[1] Because Adam and Eve were white and are the ancestors of Israel, God's chosen people, so the rationale goes, only the white race can claim to be God's "true" chosen people.

Racist hate groups also believe that Jews and minorities are conspiring to wrest control of the world from whites, who are designated by God as the world's rightful leaders. Columnist David Tyler writes that many members of hate groups—who are frequently among the lower working class and are otherwise disadvantaged and underprivileged—find it easy to accept the "claim that the Jews own more than their share of the pie and [to] blame blacks for moving up at the expense of whites."[2] Consequently, the leaders of Aryan Nations, Christian Identity, World Church of the Creator, and other racist groups teach that violence against Jews and minorities is necessary to honor God and to preserve the white race. According to Gary Greenebaum, a rabbi and the western regional director of the American Jewish Committee, hate groups are "a growing American fringe movement that is not only justifying but glorifying violence against Jews and minorities."[3]

Shifting the Blame

Racist groups allow their followers to shift the blame for their failures in life from themselves to minorities and other "enemies." White supremacists argue that they're the true "victims" because minorities are given special preferences or because there's a conspiracy among the Jews or blacks to keep the white man down. Likewise, hate groups refuse to take responsibility for the violence their rhetoric incites, shifting the blame onto their followers. As reports of a notorious hate crime hit the papers, the racist group linked to the perpetrator(s) issues a statement in which the organization maintains that it deplores violence and had nothing to do with the crime. This argument is not credible. As columnist Susan Estrich explains, "Those who taught Furrow the tenets of hatred and terrorism knew or should have known that planting such beliefs in the mind of a clearly disturbed man could lead to tragic consequences."[4] California state senator Tom Hayden concurs:

> It is a dangerous denial to believe that these acts of violence are nothing more than the work of deranged and isolated individuals. Of course, there is no single conspiracy linking [hate groups and their followers]. But there are supremacist ideologies, networks and armed groups that together create an atmosphere that stimulates and condones these violent eruptions.[5]

Leaderless Resistance

Aryan Nations, Christian Identity, World Church of the Creator, and other white supremacist groups teach their followers to hate minorities. They also maintain that violence and terrorism against minorities are the necessary means to achieve their desired ends of racial "purity" and segregation. But when their members attack minorities, the groups claim that their followers acted on their own in interpreting the groups' beliefs. This is all part of the strategy of "leaderless resistance," a plan of attack that became increasingly common during the 1990s. Hate group leaders know that as long as they call for a general revolution, and not a specific attack, their speech is protected by the Constitution. When an individual takes matters further—as Furrow did when he admitted to the FBI that the shootings were "a wake-up call to America to kill Jews"[6]—the absence of a specific plan of attack from the group legally separates the acts and speech of the hate group from those of its followers.

However, what is legal and what is right and logical are not necessarily the same thing. The Constitution does not protect words that are used to incite violence or crime, and racist groups should not be allowed to hide behind meaningless disclaimers. Their entire ideology is based on hate and violence, and when one of their members acts on that hate, the sponsoring group should be held liable as well. Furrow and others like him who commit hate crimes may act alone, but they are not solely responsible for their actions. White supremacist and other hate groups that justify and glorify violence against Jews and minorities are just as responsible. There is certainly a strong enough connection between Furrow and Aryan Nations and Christian Identity to charge them as accomplices in his crimes.

Racist hate groups and their members are dangerous. They are an immense threat to America's peace and security. They should not be allowed to hide behind constitutional protections that were not meant to safeguard such despicable behavior.

1. World Church of the Creator, "FAQ About Creativity," www.creator.org/faq.html.

2. David Tyler, "Social Inequality Fosters Resentment and Frustration Hate Groups Feed On," *New Unionist*, February 2000, p. 4.

3. Gary Greenebaum, "Racists Can Justify Anything, Even Child Murder," *Liberal Opinion Week*, August 23, 1999, p. 11.

4. Susan Estrich, "The Threat Posed by Hate Groups," *Liberal Opinion Week*, August 23, 1999, p. 11.

5. Tom Hayden, "These Aren't Isolated Acts of Violence," *Liberal Opinion Week*, August 23, 1999, p. 12.

6. Quoted in Gordon Smith and Ken Hallinan, "L.A. Shooting Suspect Held on Murder Charge," *San Diego Union-Tribune*, August 12, 1999, p. A1.

"Christian Identity and the white supremacy movement do not promote hate or advocate violence."

Racist Groups Do Not Promote Hate and Violence

Charles Lee, grand dragon of the White Camelia Knights of the Ku Klux Klan in Texas and a member of the Christian Identity white supremacy church, has been given a bad rap. Lee, who as a racialist wants nothing more than to promote and advance the white race and keep it pure and separate from other races, has been unfairly labeled as a racist hatemonger by the news media and civil rights groups such as the Anti-Defamation League (ADL) and the Southern Poverty Law Center (SPLC). Despite his views on race, Lee insists that he is not a hatemonger: "I am a Christian. I believe whites are superior to non-whites but that does not mean that I hate anyone. . . . I meet white people all the time who hate me and everything I stand for. They don't seem to realize that what I stand for is them and the entire white race. They hate me, but *I'm* supposed to be the hatemonger."[1]

Soldiers of God

Lee and other leaders of white supremacy groups—Tom Metzger of White Aryan Resistance (WAR), Matthew Hale of World Church of the Creator (WCOTC), Richard Butler of

Aryan Nations, and Pete Peters of Christian Identity—consider themselves "soldiers of God"[2] in the war to prevent the destruction of the white race through race mixing. These white supremacists admit that they are racists, or racialists, but to them the label means they are proud of the white race's culture, not that they are consumed with hatred for minorities and Jews.

As white supremacists, these men believe the white race is superior to all others, and that God commands them to keep the races pure. Charles Weisman, a noted Christian Identity preacher, quotes Scripture to support this view:

> God commanded Israel not to mix or hybridize the different kinds (species) of plants and animals (Lev. 19:19; Deut. 22:9). He also told them not to mix with other racial types or alien women (Deut. 7:1–3; Ezra 9:1–2,12; 10:10–11). This proves that different kinds [races] can reproduce but that it was not God's plan. Hybrids are the doing of man, not nature.[3]

Therefore, the tenets of Christian Identity direct its followers to keep the races as God created them: "It is the duty of every Christian to preserve God's creation and defend the order He established! . . . God did not create racially mixed people, that is man's doing through man's rejection of God's law-order of 'kind after kind.'"[4]

Separate the Races

To prevent the contamination of the white race by blacks, Hispanics, Jews, and other minorities, white separatists maintain that each race should have its own homeland. They believe that racism is an instinctive reaction in all people of all races and cannot be ignored or eradicated. In fact, they believe that inherent prejudice is responsible for racial tensions in the United States and in other nations. "If we separate races, then a lot of the other problems will disappear overnight,"[5] Metzger contends. Others outside the white supremacy movement are advocates for racial nationhood as well; Louis Farrakhan, minister and leader of the black separatist group Nation of Islam; many Native American tribes; and the Jewish state of Israel all believe they would be better off with a separate homeland. Despite the fact that white separatists do not believe integration among the races can be successful, they maintain that they can be racialists without resorting to violence against those whom they see as enemies or as inferior to the white race. Sean Haines, the leader of the Aryan Nations youth corps who has been affiliated with the group since 1989, explains how he avoids conflict: "I try to avoid situations that would bring me into confrontations. We preach vigilance, not violence."[6]

It is unfortunate that some skinheads, as many youths involved in the white supremacy movement call themselves, after the practice of shaving their heads, do not practice the vigilance needed to avoid conflict, as touted by Haines. Skinheads frequently are responsible for painting swastikas and other graffiti on buildings, distributing hate literature, and provoking violent confrontations with minorities, Jews, and homosexuals. While many skinheads believe that violence is acceptable and necessary in order to win the white separatist war, Lee and other white supremacists do not encourage the violence. According to Lee, the skinheads "get a little exuberant. They haven't matured in their faith or their beliefs, so you kind of have to take that into consideration when you talk to them. Sometimes they overdo it."[7]

Leaderless Resistance

When skinheads "overdo it," the white supremacy movement should not be blamed. The skinheads are acting on their own, under the strategy of leaderless resistance, in which individuals fight independently for the same cause. Timothy McVeigh, who was convicted of the 1995 bombing of a federal building in Oklahoma City that killed 168 civilians, was also a believer in leaderless resistance. McVeigh believed the federal government was oppressing and abusing its citizens, and he thought the bombing would rouse the American public to revolt against the government. But to blame his actions on the white supremacist movement because he had read *The Turner Diaries*, written by racialist William Pierce, who advocates blowing up government buildings to start a revolution, is ludicrous. Christian Identity preacher Pete Peters explains why such an idea should not be taken seriously in this hypothetical news release:

OKLAHOMA BOMBER HAS TIES TO THE VATICAN

A Douay Bible was found in Timothy McVeigh's getaway car, with a book mark in the book of *Judges*. The book of *Judges* is one of the most violent and bloody history books in the Bible. The Douay Bible is a Roman Catholic translation, and McVeigh—a professing Roman Catholic—is a past student of a Roman Catholic parochial school. The Pope has refused to comment, but his aids [sic] adamantly insist their's [sic] is not a religion of violence. Roman Catholicism has long been the subject of conspiracy theories which allege that Jesuit priests desire to destroy Protestants by any means possible.[8]

Just as no sane person would condemn the Roman Catholic Church for the actions of one of its followers, neither should the white supremacy movement be blamed for the actions of its followers. Matthew Hale, leader of the World Church of the Creator, argues, "The pope can't control every Catholic and I can't control every 'Creator.'"[9] Trying to link heinous acts such as the Oklahoma City bombing or the murders and attempted murders of minorities and Jews with the white supremacy movement because the perpetrators are or have been affiliated with the white supremacy movement is both immoral and irresponsible.

Although prejudice, hate, and violence between the races exists, Christian Identity, World Church of the Creator, and other established white supremacy groups do not encourage or condone hate and violence. As for those individuals with no formal affiliation with any organization in the white supremacy movement who nevertheless read and study the literature of these groups—*The Turner Diaries, National Vanguard, Stormfront*—and make their own preparations for the war they believe is imminent, there is no way the movement's leaders can predict or control their actions. Jim Stinson, a Klansman with the White Camelia in Texas, is frustrated when the news media and organizations such as the ADL and SPLC link individuals on the fringe with the white separatist groups. "You can't hold anyone responsible for that kind of thing. I mean, if McVeigh read the book *[The Turner Diaries]* and built a bomb like the one in the book ... I don't see where you can reach the conclusion [its author] Pierce put him up to it."[10]

Timothy McVeigh, convicted of bombing an Oklahoma City federal building in 1995, has been linked to the white supremacist movement.

A Double Standard

Many in the white separatist movement feel that they are persecuted and harassed for their beliefs, and object that American society empathizes with other racial groups—such as Jews and blacks—who express the same racism. White supremacists resent this double standard. Peters defends his beliefs: "The Identity belief is not a crime. . . . The Identity belief does not infringe upon anyone's life, liberty, or property. No man who chooses to believe the doctrine labeled Identity is a criminal for doing so."[11] And Christian Identity and the white supremacy movement do not promote hate or advocate violence.

1. Quoted in Howard L. Bushart, John R. Craig, and Myra Barnes, *Soldiers of God: White Supremacists and Their Holy War for America.* New York: Kensington Books, 1998, pp. 1–2.

2. Quoted in Bushart, Craig, and Barnes, *Soldiers of God*, p. 1.

3. Charles Weisman, "A Debate on Race and the Bible," n.d., http://www.seek-info.com/debate.htm.

4. Rick Savage, "Frequently Asked Questions About Creativity," n.d., www.creator.org/faq/html.

5. Quoted in Sandi Dolbee, "To White Supremacist Metzger, Racist Crusade Is 'Nothing Personal,'" *San Diego Union-Tribune*, November 10, 1995, p. E4.

6. Quoted in Brad Knickerbocker, "White Separatists Plot 'Pure' Society," *Christian Science Monitor*, April 20, 1995, p. 11.

7. Quoted in Bushart, Craig, and Barnes, *Soldiers of God*, p. 210.

8. Pete Peters, "How Far Will They Go?" n.d., www.identity.org/index.html/how_far.html.

9. Quoted in Jay Hughes, "Racist Church Membership Increases," AP Online, July 2, 2000.

10. Quoted in Bushart, Craig, and Barnes, *Soldiers of God*, p. 6.

11. Pete Peters, "The Label Identity," n.d., www.identity.org/index.html/the_label.html.

CHAPTER 2

Should Hate Speech Be Restricted?

"Rules restricting hate speech contribute to productive and welcoming environments, at home, at school, and in the workplace."

Laws Against Hate Speech Are Justified

In the early 1990s, Russ and Laura Jones, who are black, moved into a white neighborhood in St. Paul, Minnesota. Not long after their move, a group of skinheads began to terrorize them. The skinheads' campaign of intimidation began with racial slurs directed at them as they walked on the sidewalk and culminated in a burning cross in their fenced-in yard. Russ Jones describes how he felt when he awoke in the night to discover flames outside his window:

> I felt a combination of anger and fear. At first I felt anger—like someone had violated me—my space—like they were challenging me. Then I thought of my family sleeping in the next rooms and I felt fear. I was going to go out there and confront whoever was threatening us, but that would have been a pretty stupid thing to do.[1]

Jones knew, as his grandparents in the South knew, what a burning cross in a black family's yard meant: "They either meant to harm you or to put you in your place. It was a clear threat."[2]

The Power of Hate
Racists, skinheads, and hate groups understand the power of hateful words. Children are taught at an early age that "Sticks

and stones may break my bones but words will never hurt me," but they soon learn that the old saying is not true. Words *do* hurt. Not only does hate speech hurt, but it also demeans both the victim and the victim's group. According to Owen M. Fiss, author of *The Irony of Free Speech*, "Hate speech tends to diminish the victims' sense of worth. . . . When these victims speak, their words lack authority; it is as though they said nothing."[3] Hate speech therefore prevents people from participating fully in society, and society as a whole suffers. Jones explains how the skinheads' campaign of taunts and threats against his family affected them:

> [The skinheads] absolutely terrified us and the neighbors. It was awful. I felt trapped in my own home. We didn't go anywhere because I would have had to face them and could never tell what they would do. . . . These people were going to drive us out of our own home.[4]

Equality Under the Law

The fact that people can say such hurtful and demeaning things about other people shows that society does not truly recognize all people as equals. Hate speech is especially insidious because it harms not only the person it is directed at, but the entire community as well. According to Catharine MacKinnon, author of *Only Words*, the First Amendment, which guarantees freedom of speech, is on a collision course with the Fourteenth Amendment, which guarantees equality under the law. MacKinnon argues that as long as hate speech is protected by the courts, minorities will continue to be degraded by "speech of inequality."[5]

Through their actual and symbolic speech, the skinheads intended to make the Jones family feel afraid, harassed, intimidated, and demeaned, and they succeeded. Their campaign of hate speech against the Jones family continued nonstop until the federal government stepped in and charged the skinheads with violating the family's civil rights. According to Laura Jones, "The convictions themselves produced the biggest message. . . . They knew if they threatened us, they would go to jail."[6] They also learned that the right of free speech does not supercede another's right to live without fear and harassment.

As the Jones case illustrates, hate speech doesn't stop until the speaker has to pay a penalty. Banning hate speech is the only way to stop or prevent it. When hate speech is restricted, members of minorities and victimized groups feel like valued and equal members of society. Rules restricting hate speech contribute to productive and welcoming environments, at home, at school, and in the workplace.

Speech Can Be Restricted

Many people argue that hate speech should not be restricted on constitutional and other grounds. They contend that prohibiting hate speech would violate the First Amendment, which guarantees the right of freedom of speech. However, the U.S. Supreme Court has already declared that the right of free speech is not absolute. In a 1942 decision, *Chaplinsky v. New Hampshire*, the court ruled that the First Amendment does not protect "fighting words":

> It is well understood that the right of free speech is not absolute at all times and under all circumstances. There are certain well-defined and narrowly limited classes of speech, the prevention of and punishment of which have never been thought to raise any Constitutional problem. These include the lewd and obscene, the profane, the libelous, and the insulting or "fighting" words—those which by their very utterance inflict injury or tend to incite an immediate breach of the peace.[7]

The Supreme Court expanded on *Chaplinsky* ten years later in its decision in *Beauharnais v. Illinois*. In this case, a white racist was passing out leaflets that called on whites to keep blacks out of white neighborhoods. The Court ruled that if individuals could be libeled, then so could groups, and upheld a law that made it illegal to defame a race or group of people.

In *Wisconsin v. Mitchell*, the Supreme Court again agreed that free speech may be restricted. In 1989, a young black man, Todd Mitchell, and a group of friends were discussing a racist scene in the movie *Mississippi Burning*, in which a white man beats a black boy, when a young white boy walked by. Mitchell urged his friends to attack the boy. Mitchell and the other assailants were arrested; although Mitchell himself did not physically attack the boy, he was sentenced to two years in prison for his role in the assault. Mitchell received an additional sentence of five years because he selected the victim based on his race. The decision maintained that the penalty enhancement for the hate-based nature of the crime did not violate Mitchell's First Amendment rights because the speech was connected with a specific crime and "because this conduct is thought to inflict greater individual and societal harm."[8]

Helping Achieve a Hate-Free Environment

In light of these legal precedents, the city of St. Paul had no reason to doubt that its hate speech ordinance would pass constitutional muster. St. Paul designed a law to protect its citizens from hate speech—specifically symbols, graffiti, swastikas, and burning crosses—that was meant to "arouse anger, alarm or resentment in others on the basis of race, color, creed, religion or gender."[9] According to the city of St. Paul, hate speech—and the burning cross in the Jones's front yard—fell under the Court's definition of "fighting words." However, the law was overturned in 1992 in *R.A.V. v. St. Paul* when the Supreme Court ruled that the law itself was discriminatory, since it banned only "fighting words" that were motivated by the victim's race, religion, or gender. Despite being overruled, it was a good law. It made the violent bigots who terrorized the Jones family aware that their hate speech and hate crimes would not be tolerated and had legal consequences.

While St. Paul's law against hate speech was overturned, other speech codes have been upheld, especially in the workplace. In fact, in *Aguilar v. Avis Rent-a-Car*, a San Francisco judge *added* a speech code to a verdict. In this case, seventeen Latino employees charged that their Avis manager, John Lawrence, continually used ethnic slurs and derogatory comments when talking to and about them. A jury found that this hate speech was discriminatory and created a hostile workplace and awarded the workers $150,000. The judge in the case added an injunction prohibiting Lawrence from using racial epithets at work. While Avis didn't contest the award for damages, it did appeal the injunction, claiming that it infringed on the manager's right to free speech. But in 1999, the California Supreme Court upheld the lower court's ruling, finding that the right of free speech does not outweigh all other rights. The court was correct in upholding speech codes that prohibit racial slurs because such safeguards benefit society by ensuring a hate-free environment.

1. Quoted in Laura J. Lederer, "The Case of the Cross-Burning," in *The Price We Pay: The Case Against Racist Speech, Hate Propaganda, and Pornography*. Ed. Laura Lederer and Richard Delgado. New York: Hill and Wang, 1995, p. 28.

2. Quoted in Lederer, "The Case of the Cross-Burning," p. 30.

3. Owen M. Fiss, *The Irony of Free Speech*. Cambridge, MA: Harvard University Press, 1996, p. 16.

4. Quoted in Lederer, "The Case of the Cross-Burning," p. 31.

5. Catharine MacKinnon, *Only Words*. Cambridge, MA: Harvard University Press, 1993, p. 72.

6. Quoted in Lederer, "The Case of the Cross-Burning," p. 31.

7. Quoted in Maureen Harrison and Steve Gilbert, eds., *Freedom of Speech Decisions of the United States Supreme Court*. San Diego: Excellent Books, 1996, p. 13.

8. Quoted in Donald Altschiller, *Hate Crimes: A Reference Handbook*. Santa Barbara, CA: ABC-CLIO, 1999, p. 21.

9. Quoted in Harrison and Gilbert, "R.A.V. v. St. Paul," *Freedom of Speech Decisions of the United States Supreme Court*, p. 33.

"One man's hate speech is another man's political statement."

Laws Against Hate Speech Are Not Justified

Benjamin Smith, the white supremacist who killed two minorities and wounded nine more over the Fourth of July weekend in Indiana and Illinois, had been in trouble with authorities before his 1999 shooting spree. Officials at the University of Illinois in Champaign-Urbana, where Smith was enrolled, had received a variety of complaints about him during the 1997–1998 school year, including charges of domestic abuse, marijuana possession, fighting, and posting racist literature. A week before his disciplinary hearing in the spring of 1998, Smith elected to withdraw rather than face expulsion. He then enrolled at the University of Indiana in Bloomington, and immediately began placing leaflets from the White Nationalist Party and World Church of the Creator, the hate group to which he belonged, on the windshields of cars on campus and around the city. University officials met with him to discuss his racist fliers and Bloomington residents formed an organization, Bloomington United, in opposition to the leafletting. In the summer of 1998, Bloomington United organized a protest rally that drew a thousand people. At the same time, Smith held a one-man counterdemonstration in which he held up a sign that read, "No hate speech means no free speech."[1]

Hate Speech Is Free Speech

Smith's racist views are despicable, but he is right: Without hate speech, there can be no free speech. As Eric Zorn, a columnist with the *Chicago Tribune*, writes, "The concept of freedom of speech means nothing—less than nothing—if it doesn't extend to the speech of those with whom you have profound disagreements. . . . They're the ones who need it."[2] For example, many social and political movements of the 1960s, '70s, and '80s were extremely unpopular at their inception. They needed the protection of free speech in order to spread their message and their supporters often used speech that was purposefully provocative and incendiary simply to get people's attention. Charles Levendosky, an editorial page editor for the Casper, Wyoming, *Star-Tribune* and a noted First Amendment commentator, writes that the antiwar protests and the movements for desegregation, women's liberation, and Black Power, among others,

> all used inflammatory rhetoric like a blowtorch to burn a hole in the status quo. To demand that people take sides. And see the world differently. If hate speech were prohibited, socio-political movements could be crushed before they even started.[3]

These movements are perfect examples of why hate speech deserves protection. "One man's hate speech is another man's political statement," explains Levendosky. "And political commentary has—and should have—the highest First Amendment protection."[4]

Speech Codes

During the 1980s, many universities enacted speech codes to protect students from hate speech and harassment. These codes were part of a movement of "political correctness" that swept the nation during that period, in which colleges and universities went out of their way to ensure that no student was offended by any speech, actions, or even art. However, school administrators immediately discovered a problem with speech codes: They were not helping those they were designed to protect.

The goal of speech codes is apparently to protect minorities from racial slurs and epithets uttered by whites. But in the real world, that's not always how it works. In the real world, the white majority usually makes the rules. And, unfortunately, when white men rule, white men are less likely to be punished for breaking the rules. For example, the University of Michigan had a speech code against racist speech. Twenty students were charged with making racist comments before the Supreme Court struck down the code in 1989 as unconstitutional. Of those twenty, only one was prosecuted—a black student for calling another student "white trash." Codes that were designed to protect minorities from hate speech ended up being used *against* minorities more than they were applied against whites. During the 1990s, every college speech code challenged in the courts was overturned, with the result that many colleges have abandoned their attempts to restrict hate speech on campus.

Hate Speech Will Not Disappear

Without a doubt, hate speech, when directed toward specific individuals or groups, is harmful. It is demeaning and perpetuates stereotypes; it causes its targets to feel anger, fear, and a sense of powerlessness; and it damages victims' self-confidence and self-esteem. But banning hate speech will not change the attitudes or beliefs of the hatemongers. Hate will exist even if hate speech is banned. "Punishing speech is not the same thing as curing hate,"[5] contends Paul K. McMasters, the First Amendment ombudsman at the Freedom Forum, a foundation that studies issues involving freedom of speech and of the press. Hate speech does not cause bigotry, but is merely a manifestation of it. Prohibiting hate speech might also make society become blind to the fact that racism, hate, and bigotry exist.

Moreover, if racists are forced to stop spreading their message and disappear from public view, it becomes much more difficult to keep track of them and their activities. It is harder to fight a hidden enemy than one in plain sight. McMasters explains some of the benefits of keeping bigots out in the open:

> Hate speech uncovers the haters. It exposes the ignorance, fear, and incoherence in their views. It warns, prepares, and galvanizes the targets. It provides the police with suspects and the prosecutors with evidence in the event of a crime.[6]

He adds that permitting hate speech demonstrates society's tolerance of intolerance and the importance it places on freedom of speech.

Suppressing hate speech and driving hate groups and bigots underground could also be dangerous because hate and resentment grow below the surface of society. If people are forced to keep their hate bottled up instead of speaking out, the hate and tension and frustration may grow until it explodes in violence against the hated group. Allowing people to express their hate and anger via speech acts like a pressure valve and actually results in less violence. According to Stephen A. Smith, a communications professor at the University of Arkansas, keeping hate speech in the open is the best way to deal with the problem:

> Legal restrictions on hate speech only suppress the symptoms; they do not treat the underlying causes of the social disease. Applying the Band-Aid of a speech code might keep it from the sight of those who would be repulsed, but the infection would remain and fester. A better prescription would be to expose it to the air of speech and the light of reason, the healing antibiotic of counterargument.[7]

Fight Hate Speech with More Speech

Counterargument and more speech are the best responses to hate speech. Suppressing hate speech will not suppress the beliefs that motivate it—too many people share the same despicable views held by hate groups and racists about minorities, Jews, gays, women, and others. When bigots start spreading lies, racism, and illogical conclusions on the radio, television, or Internet, in leaflets and fliers, or at rallies and demonstrations, all free-thinking Americans must speak up and correct the lies in the hatemongers' inflammatory rhetoric. Racist ideas must be confronted by nonracist views. When hate speech is challenged with more speech, the audience hears more than one point of view and is more likely to analyze and scrutinize the merits and faults of each argument. James Madison, who wrote the First Amendment, was confident that when the facts are known, the truth will prevail: As he put it, "Knowledge will forever govern ignorance."[8]

1. Quoted in Eric Zorn, "Free Speech Is the Only Refuge of a Hatemonger," *Liberal Opinion Week*, July 19, 1999, p. 24.

2. Zorn, "Free Speech Is the Only Refuge of a Hatemonger," p. 24.

3. Charles Levendosky, "One Man's Hate Speech, Another's Political Speech," *Liberal Opinion Week*, August 17, 1998, p. 14.

4. Levendosky, "One Man's Hate Speech, Another's Political Speech," p. 14.

5. Paul K. McMasters, "Must a Civil Society Be a Censored Society?" *Human Rights*, Fall 1999, p. 10.

6. McMasters, "Must a Civil Society Be a Censored Society?" p. 10.

7. Stephen A. Smith, "There's Such a Thing as Free Speech, and It's a Good Thing, Too," in *Hate Speech*. Ed. Rita Kirk Whillock and David Slayden. Thousand Oaks, CA: Sage, 1995, p. 260.

8. Quoted in Josiah H. Brown, "In Memory of Free Speech," *Wall Street Journal*, November 27, 1996, p. A12.

"I doubt seriously if the writers of our Constitution and Bill of Rights intended that freedom of speech could be a way that people can spread their hate philosophy. I don't think that free speech means hate speech."

Hate Speech on the Internet Should Be Restricted

Ricky Byrdsong, a former basketball coach at Northwestern University, was out jogging with two of his children in Skokie, Illinois, in July 1999, when Benjamin Smith drove by. Smith didn't know Byrdsong, but he saw that the jogger was black, and that was enough for Smith, who was associated with the racist World Church of the Creator white supremacist group. Smith shot and killed the forty-three-year-old father in front of his children, then drove off to terrorize more people. Smith ended up killing two men, including Byrdsong, and wounding nine other people over three days before killing himself during a high-speed police chase.

Although Matthew Hale, the leader of World Church of the Creator, knew Smith personally, he denied any connection between the organization's racist beliefs and Smith's actions. Byrdsong's wife, Sherialyn, does not agree. She argues that the group's Web page and other hate sites had a profound effect on Smith:

> I believe that Ben Smith was probably greatly influenced by things that he heard and saw over the Internet,

50

because there seems to be a lot of sites where people can visit to learn about hate and hate groups, supremacist movements, and philosophies. I believe he became so brainwashed . . . that what he was learning overpowered any kind of human esteem for the lives of people who were different from himself.[1]

A Boon for Hate Groups

The development of the Internet has been a boon for white supremacist groups. Hate groups such as the World Church of the Creator, National Alliance, Stormfront, and others "have established a significant, unprecedented beachhead in the mainstream of our culture,"[2] contends Rabbi Abraham Cooper, the associate dean of the Simon Wiesenthal Center (SWC), a Jewish human rights organization that monitors anti-Semitism and other hate. Cooper testified before a congressional committee just how dangerous hate on the Internet is:

> For the first time in the history of our democracy, those promoting hate, racial violence, and terrorism have been able to do so directly into the mainstream, twenty-four hours a day, seven days a week, in an unassailable and attractive format. For them, the Internet has already succeeded beyond their wildest dreams in undermining our civil society. Taking a page from the all-too-successful game book of international terrorists, they use the Internet to inspire a social misfit in a high school, a racist lone wolf—or an unnamed, leaderless resistance cell to act out white power fantasies against blacks, Jews, or Asian Americans.[3]

Cooper's views are shared by Mark Potok, director of the Southern Poverty Law Center's *Intelligence Report*. Potok blames Internet hate sites as "the main culprit"[4] for the increase in organized hate groups.

The first hate site was established in 1995 by Don Black, an ex-convict who acquired computer skills in prison. Black acknowledges that the Internet has been "a major breakthrough"[5] for the white supremacist movement. He boasts that his hate site, Stormfront, generates between fifteen hundred and seventeen hundred hits a day during the week, and even more on weekends. "We have recruited people to our point of view, many people which we otherwise wouldn't have reached. Sites such as Stormfront, which are interactive, provide those people who are attracted to our ideas with a forum to talk to each other and to form a virtual community."[6]

Although estimates of the number of hate sites on the Internet vary, depending on who's doing the counting and what criteria are used (sites originating in the United States versus international groups or white supremacist groups versus black pride groups, for example), at any given time 300 to more than 2,000 hate websites are active. The Southern Poverty Law Center counted 305 hate sites in 1999, while a 1999 Simon Wiesenthal

Walt Handelsman. © Tribune Information Services, Inc. All rights reserved. Reprinted with permission.

Center report listed some 2,800 problematic sites. Regardless of the total, all observers agree that the ranks of hate sites are increasing dramatically—sometimes doubling—every year. Cooper estimates that due to the increase in online hate, the staff at the Simon Wiesenthal Center spends about 70 percent of its time monitoring hate groups' Internet sites.

The Threat Is Real

The threat posed by hate groups and their websites is very real. Racists and white supremacist groups use their Web pages to recruit and propagandize anyone who might be drawn to their cause. Children and youth are especially attractive to hate groups because they are the movement's future leaders. Some hate sites have Web pages designed specifically for younger children, with games and racist-themed pages to print and color.

Hate sites are also dangerous for teens, many of whom have not yet developed critical thinking skills and mature judgment; many are thus unable to distinguish between truth and distortions, lies, and disinformation on the websites. According to Cooper, "The Internet can give the erroneous impression that all information is of the same value. . . . Information needs context to be understood, especially by young people."[7]

Hate sites present a difficult dilemma for parents, hate group monitors, and legislators. Hate is dangerous, as Sherialyn Byrdsong is well aware. She believes hate on the Internet has a greater impact on people than fliers, leaflets, and other kinds of hate propaganda. She notes that racists can log on to the Internet anytime and

> just be fed doses of hate messages. It's free, it's available. It's so accessible. Unfortunately, the Internet can be used in a negative way much more powerfully than it can in a positive way, in the sense that it can take someone's life, as it did my husband's life.[8]

For this reason, Byrdsong believes hate on the Internet should be banned. "I doubt seriously if the writers of our Constitution and Bill of Rights intended that freedom of speech could be a way that people can spread their hate philosophy. I don't think that free speech means hate speech."[9]

The Simon Wiesenthal Center has had some success in banning hate speech on the Internet in Canada, Great Britain, and Germany, where hate speech is illegal. In the United States, however, the center must resort to other tactics. It has submitted a list of hate sites to the sites' Internet service providers with the hope that the ISPs will then kick them off. Several ISPs have guidelines covering the content on their subscribers' sites. For example, Geocities prohibits "blatant expressions of racism and hatred,"[10] and Internet attorney David Kramer maintains that such restrictions do not violate the First Amendment's guarantee of free speech: "The relationship between an ISP and subscribers is purely contractual. They are not a government entity and aren't bound by restrictions of the First Amendment. In fact, in most of the agreements between ISPs and their subscribers, there's a clause that allows the ISP to do whatever it chooses."[11]

Filters

A few Internet service providers also have programmable filters that parents and schools can use to block access to websites that feature objectionable material, such as racist Web pages or pornography. In addition to ISP filters, there are many software filter programs available for purchase by parents and schools to prevent children from gaining access to offensive sites. The Anti-Defamation League has developed a software filter specifically designed to block hate sites from a user's computer. Mark Edelman, the director of marketing and communications for the ADL, explains why his organization decided to develop filter software: "We are very much for free speech. This particular product is not meant to prevent speech. It's solely designed for parents who have a certain right to protect their own children from hate."[12]

Although filters are imperfect, they are a useful tool for parents and schools to use until the Supreme Court recognizes the danger presented by hate speech on the Internet and allows local and state governments to ban it.

1. Quoted in Lisa Napoli, "Web of Hate," *MSNBC.com*, September 12, 1999, www.msnbc.com/news/458895.asp?0na=22076X0&cpl=1.

2. Quoted in Michael Marriott, "Rising Tide: Sites Born of Hate," *New York Times*, March 18, 1999, p. D4.

3. Abraham Cooper, testimony on "Hate on the Internet," before the Senate Committee on the Judiciary, September 14, 1999.

4. Quoted in Ros Davidson, "Web of Hate," *Salon.com*, October 16, 1998, www.salon.com/news/1998/10/16newsa.html.

5. Quoted in Toby Eckert, "Hate Groups Find Web Useful Tool to Spread Word," *San Diego Union-Tribune*, November 9, 1999, p. A11.

6. Quoted in Ted Koppel, transcript, "Hate and the Internet," *Nightline*, January 13, 1997, http://www.stormfront.org/dblack/nightline011398.htm.

7. Quoted in David Hipschman, "Dealing with Hate on the Net," *WebReview*, November 10, 1995, http://webreview.com/nov10/features/hate/index.html.

8. Quoted in Napoli, "Web of Hate."

9. Quoted in Napoli, "Web of Hate."

10. Quoted in Jennifer Oldham, "Wiesenthal Center Compiles List of Hate-Based Websites," *Los Angeles Times*, December 18, 1997, p. A26.

11. Quoted in Oldham, "Wiesenthal Center Compiles List of Hate-Based Websites," p. A26.

12. Quoted in Oldham, "Wiesenthal Center Compiles List of Hate-Based Websites," p. A26.

"The Internet helps strengthen the marketplace of ideas, in which reason, goodwill, and tolerance will triumph over prejudice, hate, and intolerance."

Hate Speech on the Internet Should Not Be Restricted

The Anti-Defamation League, a hate-monitoring group that fights anti-Semitism and bigotry, released a report in which it calls the National Alliance "the single most organized hate group in the United States today" and the "largest and most active neo-Nazi organization in the nation."[1] According to the ADL, the National Alliance increased its membership by almost 50 percent in 1999—up to fifteen hundred dues-paying members—after enduring a stagnant membership roster for ten years. The report states that the dramatic increase in NA membership is due to its aggressive incorporation of the Internet into its recruiting and propaganda activities.

If the number of members reported is true (the National Alliance isn't saying), these figures and allegations are troubling for what they indicate about race relations in the United States. However, it's important to keep the rise in NA membership in perspective. Even if the National Alliance does have fifteen hundred dues-paying members, that number is very tiny compared with the population of the United States—currently at about 250 million. Fifteen hundred racists are about .0006 percent of the population, hardly enough to start a race war.

Internet Hate Sites

The National Alliance website is one of the more sophisticated and technically advanced hate sites on the Internet. Estimates of the total number of Internet hate sites range from a low of 305 to a high of 2,800, depending on who is counting and what criteria are used to define "hate site." The Simon Wiesenthal Center, which offers the number 2,800, includes any Web page, based in any country, that is biased against any group, including whites, blacks, Jews, gays, and pro-choice activists, whereas the Southern Poverty Law Center, citing 305 hate sites, includes only organized hate groups based in the United States. Allowing for as many as 2,800 hate sites on the Internet, that's still an infinitesimal number compared to the millions, perhaps billions, of Web pages available in cyberspace. Film critic Roger Ebert helps put the number of hate sites in perspective. He estimates that hate sites are 1,000 times less popular than graphic porn websites, which take up about 1.5 percent of an estimated 800 million Web pages. Ebert contends that regular visitors to hate sites number only in the hundreds, and that hit counts are often exaggerated by both those who monitor racist Web pages, because they need to make their work seem important, and by the hatemongers themselves, who want to make their groups seem more dangerous than they are. Therefore, he concludes, "Racist creeps with hate sites must face the inevitable reality that most of the visitors are none other than themselves."[2]

Ebert is not alone in his belief that the media overplay the importance of hate sites and the number of visitors they receive. Ken McVay, who campaigns tirelessly against Internet hate and Holocaust revisionists—those who claim that there is no proof that 6 million Jews died during World War II—believes that the media exaggerates the presence and power of racist neo-Nazis, skinheads, white supremacists, and others:

> For all their vitriol, these people are only a tiny handful of the 30–40 million users on the Internet. I am weary of seeing their activities blown out of proportion. . . .

We are dealing with a few dozen cynical activists, trolling the net for money and cannon fodder. Even if *all* of the estimated 20,000 or so Fascists on the continent became active on the Net they *still* would represent no more than a small ripple in the Internet pond. In spite of that, the press continues to sensationalize their presence, using it as an excuse for black headlines, and the Canadian and American governments dutifully blather about "controlling the Internet," presumably for "our own good."[3]

The Marketplace of Ideas

"Controlling the Internet" may sound like a good idea, but in reality trying to censor or shut down offensive websites would harm society and benefit hate groups. According to columnist Scott Rosenberg:

> Shutting down Websites that publish idiotic racist and anti-Semitic ideas might give people a sense of having struck a blow for sanity. But it's not very practical. Close down one Website and another five spring up. And it tends to backfire, giving racists a chance to pose as martyrs in the cause of free speech.[4]

Rosenberg adds that many people have an irrational fear that racist, hate-based speech will make converts of anyone who is exposed to it. What they don't take into account is the theory of the "marketplace of ideas," first proposed by philosopher John Stuart Mill, in which all ideas, good and bad, are presented to the public who then "vigorously and earnestly"[5] debate them. The good ideas survive, while the bad ideas disappear. In this case, hate speech is a bad idea and it will not make the cut in the arena of public debate.

Computer software that prevents access to racist and hate-filled websites thwarts the marketplace of ideas and prevents open discussion of hate. Pretending that hate does not exist does not make it so. Software filters may be a useful tool, but parents should not rely on them because many children are capable of getting around the filters. Instead of hoping that their children do not come across websites like National Alliance, Stormfront, or World Church of the Creator, parents should discuss the ideas that fuel these sites with their children. Joseph T. Roy, editor of the Southern Poverty Law Center's *Intelligence Report*, testified before a Senate committee that the best response to Internet hate speech is more speech:

> The only real inoculation [against hate on the Internet] is communication. Parents need to talk to their children about these sites and what they represent. Hate sites that claim there was no Holocaust can serve as a catalyst for a discussion of what Nazi Germany was all about. The racism found on white supremacist sites can spark a family exchange about the nature of racism and the need to celebrate, not fear, racial and other differences. . . . The alternative is to try to ignore these sites and to hope your child does not come across them—a hope that is increasingly unrealistic. History shows us that ignoring ugly social problems like racism does not make them go away. On the contrary, burying one's head in the sand is a sure way to guarantee the spread of hate.[6]

The Internet helps strengthen the marketplace of ideas, in which reason, goodwill, and tolerance will triumph over prejudice, hate, and intolerance.

1. Anti-Defamation League, "Explosion of Hate: The Growing Danger of the National Alliance," 1998, www.adl.org/Frames/front_explosion_of_hate.html.
2. Roger Ebert, "When the Web Is in the Headline," *ZDNet*, October 1999, www.zdnet.com/yil/content/columnists/ebert9910.html.

3. Quoted in Jonathan Wallace and Mark Mangan, *Sex, Laws, and Cyberspace: Freedom and Regulation on the Frontiers of the Online Revolution*. New York: Henry Holt, 1996, pp. 245–46.

4. Scott Rosenberg, "The Web Can't Make Racists," *Salon.com*, July 9, 1999, www.salon.com/tech/col/rose/1999/07/09/.

5. Quoted in Rosenberg, "The Web Can't Make Racists."

6. Joseph T. Roy, "Hate on the Internet," testimony before the Senate Committee on the Judiciary, September 14, 1999.

CHAPTER 3

Are Laws Against Hate Crimes Necessary?

"A hate crime law would ensure that people are not victimized simply because of how they look, what religion they practice, or who they love."

Hate Crime Laws Are Necessary

Each year has its notorious hate crime incidents. June 1998 saw the dragging death of James Byrd Jr., a black man from Jasper, Texas, by white racists. Not long after, in October 1998, Matthew Shepard, a gay college student, was robbed, beaten into a coma, tied to a fence, and left to die near Laramie, Wyoming. In July 1999, Benjamin Smith went on a racially motivated shooting spree, killing a black former basketball coach and a Korean college student and wounding nine other minorities in Indiana and Illinois. A month later in Los Angeles, white supremacist Buford Furrow shot and injured five people—including three children—at a Jewish community center, and then killed a Filipino mail carrier, Joseph Ileto. In March 2000, Ronald Taylor, who is black, shot and killed three white men and wounded two others in Wilkinsburg, Pennsylvania. Eight weeks later, Richard Bauhammers, who is white, killed five minorities and wounded a sixth near Pittsburgh, Pennsylvania.

These horrifying murders and assaults are fundamentally different from other violent crimes. They are hate crimes: The victims were chosen only because they were black, white, Asian, Jewish, or gay. Hate crimes are particularly devastating because they are intended to terrorize as well as physically harm the individual. Hate crimes make the victim feel isolated and unprotected; studies have shown that hate crimes have a greater and longer-lasting psychological impact than other crimes. Research also has found that the assailants in hate crimes are more violent and inflict more serious injuries on their victims than the perpetrators of ordinary assaults do.

The Damaging Effects of Hate Crimes

Hate crimes have a damaging effect on society as well. Senator Edward Kennedy of Massachusetts describes hate crimes as "modern day lynchings"[1] because their purpose is to threaten and terrorize not only the individual but the victim's entire minority group. Thus, a seemingly isolated act of violence can devastate a community and, in the most notorious cases, the entire nation. If society does not step in to reassure the targeted group that such acts will not be tolerated, relations between the victim group and the rest of society may deteriorate irreparably. Kennedy and Arlen Specter, the Republican

Postal workers grieve during the funeral service of Joseph Ileto, a Filipino mail carrier killed by Buford Furrow.

senator from Pennsylvania who cosponsored federal hate crimes legislation with Kennedy in 1997, explain why hate crimes are so much more serious than other types of crime: "Random street crimes don't provoke riots; hate crimes can and sometimes do."[2]

History shows that, if the attacking group believes their actions are supported by the community at large, the results can be disastrous. The Holocaust against the Jews during World War II and the genocide of the ethnic Albanians in Kosovo and Muslims in Bosnia are proof that hate, left unchecked, can escalate into widespread violence and terror.

Messages of hate and intimidation also wreak havoc on the community because hate crimes endanger the principles the United States was founded on. As the editors of the *Los Angeles Times* write, hate crimes are "blows against the ideals of equality that this nation should hold most sacred."[3] When someone is beaten or killed because of his or her race, religion, or sexual orientation, it demonstrates the poor state of civil rights in America. A hate crime law would ensure that people are not victimized simply because of how they look, what religion they practice, or who they love.

A Necessary Law

Hate crime laws define which groups have historically suffered victimization and discrimination and set guidelines to severely punish criminals who specifically target these groups. Because of the devastating effect of hate crimes on both the victims and society, those who commit hate crimes should receive stiffer sentences than other criminals. Penalty enhancement laws, which increase the severity of the sentence given to someone convicted of a hate crime, send a message to racists and bigots that society will not tolerate crimes that are committed because of the victim's race, religion, gender, or sexual orientation.

Penalty enhancement in sentencing is not unusual. Society has long considered a criminal's motive and intent in the sentencing process. For example, motive and intent are important when deciding whether to charge a defendant with assault or aggravat-

Gary Markstein. Reprinted by permission of Copley News Service.

ed assault, or when deciding whether a homicide is a case of self-defense, manslaughter, second-degree murder, or first-degree murder. Penalty enhancement laws would allow society to express its outrage over hate crimes.

A federal hate crimes law is needed to expand the definition of what groups should be protected from hate crimes. A law passed during the civil rights era made it illegal to "injure, oppress, threaten, or intimidate"[4] a person because of the victim's race, color, religion, or national origin. This law needs to be expanded to include crimes that are committed on the basis of gender, sexual orientation, and disability. Many of the most vicious hate crimes committed in recent years have been committed against homosexuals or those whom the attackers believed to be homosexual. The federal hate crimes law should be expanded to include these groups because, as Kennedy argues, "The federal government . . . has a role in preventing violence against other disadvantaged groups who have historically been subject to abuse."[5] Former president Bill Clinton, who had pushed Congress to expand the federal hate crimes law since 1997, agrees, adding, "All Americans deserve protection from hate."[6]

The Federal Government Can Help

As hate groups exploit the Internet to spread their influence and message across state lines, more and more hate crimes are being committed by individuals who have ties to white supremacist organizations such as Aryan Nations, World Church of the Creator, Christian Identity, and others. The federal government can investigate and prosecute hate crimes committed by hate groups and their members more effectively than individual states can, yet the federal government lacks legal jurisdiction. Eric Holder Jr., the deputy attorney general for the United States, testified before Congress on why he believes a federal hate crimes law is necessary. According to Holder, a federal hate crimes law would

> authorize the federal government to share its law enforcement resources, forensic expertise, and civil rights experience with state and local officials. And in rare circumstances where state or local officials are unable or unwilling to bring appropriate criminal charges in state court, or where federal law or procedure is significantly better suited to the vindication of the federal interest—the United States must be able to bring federal civil rights charges. In these special cases, the public is served when, after consultation with state and local authorities, prosecutors have a federal alternative as an option.[7]

A federal hate crimes law would give the government the ability and authority to protect Americans from hate crimes.

Federal law prohibits the government's participation in prosecuting hate crimes unless the victim was engaged in one of six federally protected activities: voting, enrolling in or attending public school, serving on a jury, applying for employment or working, traveling or engaging in interstate commerce, or participating in a program, facility, or activity provided by any state or local government. For example, the government was able to provide resources for the prosecution of a hate crime murder that was committed on a public street in Lubbock, Texas, in 1994 because the government provided the funds to build the street. However, if the skinhead perpetrators had murdered their victim inside a house, the federal government would have been unable to help. Having to make such a distinction on where the crime takes place before the federal government can help just "doesn't make sense," Clinton argued. "It shouldn't matter where the murder was committed. It was still a hate crime. And the resources of the federal government were needed."[8]

Hate Will Not Be Tolerated

A hate crimes law is necessary for several reasons. It will ensure that all Americans, whatever their race, religion, gender, sexual orientation, or disability, are protected from hate crimes. It will allow the federal government to assist state governments with hate crime investigations and prosecutions. And perhaps most important, it will let bigots and racists know that hate is not acceptable. In a meeting with law enforcement officials, Attorney General Janet Reno emphasized why hate crime laws are so important. Hate crime laws "let us continue to speak against haters and hatred," she explained. "Haters are cowards and when confronted they so often back down. When we are silent, they are emboldened."[9] Hate crime laws are a means of speaking out and letting haters know that hate will not be tolerated.

1. Edward Kennedy, "Statement of Senator Edward M. Kennedy: Hate Crimes Prevention Act Amendment," June 16, 2000, www.senate.gov/~kennedy/statements/00/06/2000620E04.html.

2. Edward M. Kennedy and Arlen Specter, "When Combating Hate Should Be a Federal Fight," *Washington Post*, December 1, 1997, p. A25.

3. *Los Angeles Times*, "Tackling the Haters," July 21, 1999, p. B6.

4. Quoted in Wyn Craig Wade, *The Fiery Cross: The Ku Klux Klan in America*. New York: Oxford University Press, 1987, p. 444.

5. Edward Kennedy, "Bill Summary of the Hate Crimes Prevention Act Amendment," June 19, 2000, www.senate.gov/~kennedy/statements/00/06/2000620E14.html.

6. Bill Clinton, remarks by the president at the White House Conference on Hate Crimes, Washington, D.C., November 10, 1997, www.whitehouse.gov/uri-res/I2R?urn:pdi://oma. eop.gov.us/1997/11/12/1.text.1.

7. Eric H. Holder Jr., testimony before the Committee on the Judiciary, U.S. House of Representatives, Concerning Hate Crimes, August 4, 1999, www.usdoj/gov/dag/testimony/ dagjudic080499.htm.

8. Bill Clinton, remarks by the president on Hate Crimes, April 25, 2000, www.pub.whitehouse. gov/uri-res/I2R?urn:pdi://oma.eop.gov.us/2000/4/26/8.text.1.

9. Janet Reno, "Attorney General Reno Delivers Statement on Hate Crimes," April 25, 2000, wwws.elibrary.com.

"Only when attitudes have changed . . . will behavior finally start to change. A hate crimes law won't do it."

Hate Crime Laws Are Unnecessary

Whenever a hate crime makes the national news, such as the murders of James Byrd Jr. in Jasper, Texas, and Matthew Shepard in Laramie, Wyoming, the knee-jerk reaction of civil rights activists, the media, and liberal politicians is always the same: Pass a federal hate crimes law. A hate crimes law will prevent hate crimes, they claim. Hate crime laws are of two types. One defines which groups will receive "special" protection so that any crime committed against them can be labeled a "hate crime." The other is a penalty enhancement law, which requires that a defendant receive a stiffer sentence if it can be proved that the victim was chosen due to prejudice against his or her race, religion, national origin, and sometimes gender, disability, or sexual orientation. Congress passed a federal sentencing enhancement act in 1994 that increased the penalty for a federal crime by an average of one-third if the crime was motivated by hatred of a victim's race, color, religion, national origin, or ethnicity. Since then, Congress has been trying to expand the definition of a hate crime to include victims who are selected due to their gender, sexual orientation, or disability. If these traits are included in the federal hate crimes law, or if states pass such a law, then more people will be protected from hate crimes, civil rights advocates claim. But hate crime laws, whether at the state or federal level, are not necessary.

Two Notorious Examples

Supporters of hate crime laws condemned the lack of such laws in Texas and Wyoming when Byrd and Shepard were murdered. Byrd, a black man, was tied by his ankles to a pickup truck and dragged to his death in June 1998 by three white men who had ties to white supremacist groups. A few months later, gay rights advocates demanded the passage of a hate crimes law in Wyoming after Shepard, a gay college student, was robbed, beaten, tied to a fence, and left to die in October 1998. Hate crimes law supporters imply that Byrd and Shepard would still be alive if Texas and Wyoming had had hate crime laws. Evidently the editors of the *New York Times* believe a hate crimes law would have made a difference in Shepard's life:

> He died in a coma yesterday, in a state without a hate-crimes law. Its legislature had rejected the latest attempt to pass one in February [1998]. . . . His death makes clear the need for hate-crime laws to protect those who survive and punish those who attack others.[1]

Not a Deterrent

Unfortunately, such reasoning is faulty. James Byrd's and Matthew Shepard's murders, as heinous as they were, would not have been prevented if their states had had a hate crimes law on the books. For example, Indiana and Illinois both have hate crime laws, but that didn't stop Benjamin Smith, a white supremacist, from killing two minorities and wounding nine more in a hate-filled shooting spree in July 1999 in Bloomington and Skokie. California has a hate crimes law, and yet Buford Furrow, another white supremacist, shot children in a Jewish community center and killed a Filipino mail carrier in Los Angeles in August 1999. Hate crime laws cannot protect from harm those who are the subject of discrimination, no matter what the editors of the *New York Times* believe.

The violent acts that are included in hate crime statutes are crimes that are already prosecuted under state criminal codes.

Murder is murder. Designating Byrd's or Shepard's murder as a hate crime rather than an "ordinary" crime does not change the fact that both men are still dead. Nor does it mean that law enforcement and the judiciary will prosecute their cases any more diligently.

Crime and Punishment

The second claim in the *New York Times* editorial—that hate crime laws are necessary to ensure that those who commit hate crimes are properly punished—isn't a valid argument either. In Texas, a state known to aggressively carry out the death penalty, two of Byrd's killers were sentenced to death, the third to life in prison. Nor would a hate crimes law have made a difference for Shepard's killers in Wyoming, both of whom were sentenced to life in prison. These murderers all received the harshest penalty available under the law. But evidently being sentenced to the chair or life in prison isn't enough for the *New York Times*. Richard Dooling, a lawyer and author, explains what must be on some people's minds when they argue for hate crime laws:

The site of Matthew Shepard's brutal attack in Laramie, Wyoming. Shepard was beaten, tied to the fence, and left to die.

Texas's death penalty apparently isn't harsh enough for this kind of crime; we need a federal hate-crimes bill to send a message. Now white supremacists will know they can't get off so easy. They will receive enhanced penalties under federal law, even if retribution must be administered in the afterlife.[2]

Since we all know you can't kill someone twice or punish him after his death, hate crime laws are therefore redundant and unnecessary.

Thought Control

If hate crime legislation becomes the law of the land, then every trial could potentially become an examination of the defendant's thoughts and beliefs. For example, during a trial in Ohio, the prosecutor attempted to prove a campground dispute was the result of racial animosity by maintaining that because the defendant wasn't a close friend of his black neighbor, he was prejudiced against blacks. Despite testifying that he did have black friends, the accused was confronted with such questions as: "And you lived next door [to her] for nine years and you don't even know her first name? Never had dinner with her? Never gone out and had a beer with her? You don't associate with her, do you? All these black people that you have described that are your friends, I want you to give me one person, just one who was really a good friend of yours."[3] Under hate crime laws, the limits of relevant evidence would be expanded to include what books the accused read, the organizations he or she belonged to, and whether the defendant had a diverse range of friends. Every action and inaction would become suspect, and interrogations and prosecutions could become routine if the nation adopts hate crime laws.

But perhaps most importantly, how can anyone *know* what someone else was thinking during the commission of a crime, and then be able to *prove* it? And even if you could prove that hate was the motivation for a crime, it is unconstitutional to punish him for it. Sentencing a criminal with extra punishment for his beliefs while punishing him for his actions violates the First Amendment's guarantee of free speech. Thus, hate crime laws are a form of thought control. Hateful thought will have become a criminal activity, which is the first step toward a totalitarian government.

No other crime merits an enhanced sentence based on the criminal's thoughts. Frank Morriss, a contributing editor for the weekly Catholic newspaper the *Wanderer*, notes that sentences are not enhanced if an embezzler hates his employer, or if a bank robber hates bankers. There is only one judge of a person's thoughts, he maintains: "God has the right to judge on the basis of our motives; it is an invasion of our personal freedom of will for government to do so."[4] Giving the government such power over our thoughts and ideas threatens our rights to live and think as we please.

What Is Needed

Hate crime laws are unnecessary, ineffective, and dangerous. When bigots act on their hate and prejudice, then their crimes should be vilified and punished as the law requires. But law enforcement and judicial officials must continue to diligently prosecute *all* crimes, whether or not they are based on hate. And instead of passing new hate crime laws, Americans need to loudly and forcefully condemn such despicable acts of violence. Only when attitudes have changed toward minorities, homosexuals, women, and others who are the subject of discrimination will behavior finally start to change. A hate crimes law won't do it.

1. *New York Times*, "Murdered for Who He Was," October 13, 1998, p. A22.
2. Richard Dooling, "Punish Crime, Not Hate," *Wall Street Journal*, July 20, 1998, p. A18.
3. Quoted in George Will, "Hate Crimes: An Extension of Identity Politics," *Conservative Chronicle*, October 21, 1998, p. 27.
4. Frank Morriss, "Senate Vote on Hate Crimes Sweeps Aside Serious Considerations," *Wanderer*, August 5, 1999, p. 4.

"The Supreme Court ruled that additional sentences for hate crimes are appropriate and constitutional because hate crimes are 'thought to inflict greater individual and societal harm.'"

Penalty Enhancement Laws Are Constitutional

Hate crimes—crimes in which the victims are selected on the basis of their race, religion, ethnicity, and in some states, gender, sexual orientation, or disability—are a serious threat to the American ideals of equality and the freedom to live without fear. Hate crimes are acts of terrorism designed to instill fear and a sense of isolation and vulnerability in their victims and in the victims' communities. People who feel that they are not safe from acts of discriminatory violence become fearful, angry, and suspicious of other groups. When a community feels threatened, its members may lash out against perceived oppressors. Thus begins an escalating cycle of retaliation.

Because hate crimes present a greater danger to the safety of the community than crimes without the element of hate, the government should punish these crimes more harshly. Hate crime laws are an effective and constitutional weapon in the war against violent discrimination. Hate crime laws define which characteristics, such as race, religion, and ethnicity, deserve protected status, and then decree that offenders whose crimes were motivated by bias receive an enhanced penalty.

A Duty and an Obligation

The Supreme Court agrees that hate is evil and that the government has a duty to prohibit it. It ruled in 1984 in *Roberts v. United States Jaycees* that

> acts of invidious discrimination . . . cause unique evils that government has a compelling interest to prevent—wholly apart from the point of view such conduct may transmit. Accordingly, like violence or other types of potentially expressive activities that produce special harms distinct from their communicative impact, such practices are entitled to no constitutional protection.[1]

Therefore, the government has a duty and an obligation to protect its citizens by severely punishing acts of discriminatory violence.

Hate Crime Laws and Free Speech

A decade later in another hate crime case, *Wisconsin v. Mitchell*, the Supreme Court went further in its efforts to protect American citizens. Todd Mitchell, the black defendant, was convicted of inciting a group of black friends to beat up a white boy who was walking past by yelling, "Do you all feel hyped up to move on some white people? You want to f— somebody up? There goes a white boy; go get him."[2] Mitchell's two-year sentence was increased to seven years because he intentionally selected the victim on the basis of his race. Mitchell appealed his additional punishment, claiming that it violated his right to free speech. The Supreme Court upheld the constitutionality of the state's penalty enhancement law, ruling that "a physical assault is not by any stretch of the imagination expressive conduct protected by the First Amendment."[3] In this decision, the Supreme Court agreed that the enhanced penalty was due to the defendant's conduct—his crime of aggravated battery—and not due to his thoughts or beliefs.

Hate crime laws do not punish speech; people still have the right to express their view on any topic, no matter how contemptible that view is. But when speech turns into action or when a criminal selects a victim based on race or religion or other characteristics, then hate crime laws are appropriate. In Mitchell's case, the Supreme Court ruled that additional sentences for hate crimes are appropriate and constitutional because hate crimes are "thought to inflict greater individual and societal harm."[4]

Motive and Intent

Critics of hate crime laws contend that the laws go too far by inferring a discriminatory motive. However, law enforcement and the judicial system routinely determine motive and intent in investigating a crime or deciding what class of crime an offender should be charged with. Although every life has value, some deaths are avenged more severely than others. For example, a person who kills a police officer will receive a harsher sentence than someone who kills a friend during a drunken brawl. Society accepts the inequality of the sentences because allowing people to murder law enforcement officials with impunity threatens the stability of society. Likewise, hate crimes threaten social stability and equal rights and therefore deserve to be more severely punished.

The Supreme Court also supports the use of motive in determining a criminal's sentence. It ruled in *Wisconsin v. Mitchell* that motive may be properly considered when passing sentence on a defendant:

> In determining what sentence to impose, sentencing judges have traditionally considered a wide variety of factors in addition to evidence bearing on guilt, including a defendant's motive for committing the offense. While it is equally true that a sentencing judge may not take into consideration a defendant's abstract beliefs, however obnoxious to most people, the Constitution does not erect a *per se* barrier to the admission of evidence concerning one's beliefs and

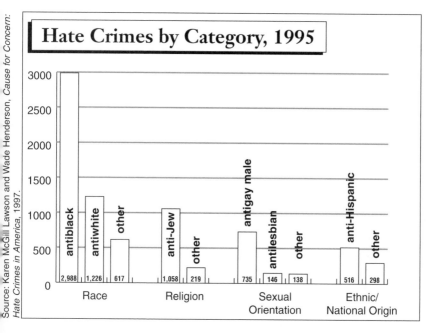

Source: Karen McGill Lawson and Wade Henderson, *Cause for Concern: Hate Crimes in America*, 1997.

Hate Crimes by Category, 1995

associations at sentencing simply because they are protected by the First Amendment.[5]

A judge may not give a defendant a harsher sentence merely because he is a white supremacist; however, if the white supremacist's desire to provoke a race war causes him to choose his victim based on race, then his motive and intent may properly be considered when handing down a sentence.

Unequal Protection

Hate crime laws also ensure that all Americans are guaranteed equal protection under the law as set forth in the Fourteenth Amendment. Hate crime laws are necessary because historically, some groups of citizens—most notably blacks and Jews—have been the focus of attacks based solely on their personal characteristics, such as race or religion. As the editors of the *Atlanta Constitution* argue:

> Hate-crime legislation doesn't create "special" groups or punish mere thoughts. Rather, it recognizes reality: Some minorities are consistently singled out for

attacks launched with fists, guns, and other weapons. Hate-crime laws don't limit speech or thought; instead, they curb the violence intended to silence certain groups.[6]

The editors add that during the first half of the twentieth century, blacks were frequently the subject of lynchings in the South. Since murder was already illegal, it could be argued that antilynching laws were unnecessary and gave special protection to minorities. But since the police and judges routinely ignored the law when blacks were murdered by whites, the editors contend that antilynching laws were necessary to raise awareness of and stop the hate-motivated killings: "The push for anti-lynching laws helped dramatically reduce the violence."[7] Hate crime laws follow the same logic; they prohibit and punish conduct that is already outlawed, but serve to raise awareness of hate crimes and reduce the violence against a group of people. For example, in response to an epidemic of black church arsons in the South during the early 1990s, Congress passed the Church Arson Prevention Act, which increased the penalties for church arson and desecration. The *Atlanta Constitution* editors contend that "that law did not create 'special rights' for church members. It simply recognized that churches are being targeted for attacks and that stiffer penalties are needed."[8]

Hate crime laws allow all Americans to live without fear. According to Senator Edward Kennedy, "No Americans should feel that they are second class citizens because Congress refuses to protect them against hate crimes."[9]

Upheld as Constitutional

Hate crime laws have been shown to reduce and prevent hate crimes. These laws are necessary and the Supreme Court has upheld them as a constitutional means of controlling and preventing hate crimes. Howard P. Berkowitz, national chairman of the Anti-Defamation League, sums up why he supports hate crime laws:

They only punish acts of violence; they neither condemn private beliefs nor chill constitutionally protected speech. The statutes guarantee that perpetrators of bias crimes will be punished in proportion to the seriousness of the crimes they have committed. The laws protect all Americans, allowing them to walk the streets safe in the knowledge that their community will not tolerate violent bigotry.[10]

1. Quoted in Brian Levin, "Does America Need a Federal Hate-Crime Law? Yes: Hate Crimes Are Especially Threatening to Their Victims and to Our Pluralistic Democracy," *Insight*, November 23, 1998, p. 26.

2. *Wisconsin v. Mitchell*, (92-515), 508 U.S. 47 (1993), http://supct.law.cornell.edu/supct/html/92-515.ZO.html.

3. *Wisconsin v. Mitchell*.

4. *Wisconsin v. Mitchell*.

5. *Wisconsin v. Mitchell*.

6. *Atlanta Constitution*, "A Tool Against Terrorism," October 19, 1998, p. 6A.

7. *Atlanta Constitution*, "Targeting Hate Crimes," February 22, 1999, p. 8A.

8. *Atlanta Constitution*, "Targeting Hate Crimes."

9. Edward M. Kennedy, "Statement of Senator Edward M. Kennedy on the Hate Crimes Prevention Act Amendment to the DoD Authorization Bill," June 1, 2000, www.senate.gov/~kennedy/statements/00/06/2000620E12.html.

10. Howard P. Berkowitz, "Q: Are Hate-Crime Laws in Keeping with a Free Society? Yes: Such Laws Send a Powerful Message to Racists and Bigots Everywhere," *Insight*, September 20, 1999, p. 43.

"Because all crimes are rooted in hatred, it is wrong, illogical, and unconstitutional to punish those that are characterized as 'hate crimes' more heavily than others."

Penalty Enhancement Laws Are Unconstitutional

Following the brutal murder of Matthew Shepard, a gay college student who was robbed, beaten into a coma, lashed to a fence, and left to die in Laramie, Wyoming, in October 1998, gay rights activists howled for a hate crime law to protect other gays from such violent bigotry. Wyoming is one of nine states that have resisted the national trend of passing hate crime laws—laws that ban derogatory speech and conduct directed at specific groups and that tack on an additional penalty to the sentences of criminals who are convicted of committing a hate crime.

Hate Crime Laws Are Problematic

Though in theory such laws are commendable—who, after all, is in favor of hate crimes?—hate crime laws are problematic for several reasons. Besides the fact that banning hate crimes does not prevent them (just as making robbery and murder illegal does not stop people from mugging and killing others), hate crime and penalty enhancement laws are clearly unconstitutional. As the editors of the *New Republic* argue, these laws create a legal distinction between someone who kills a gay man because he hates gays and someone who kills a gas-station attendant in order to steal from his cash register. To create such a distinction in effect penalizes some criminals more harshly, not because of their deeds, but because of their beliefs.[1]

The government has no right to punish people for what they say, read, or believe, or for what organizations they belong to, yet this is the purpose of hate crime laws. If a criminal can be sentenced to additional years in prison because he assaulted a black man because he believes whites are superior to blacks, then it won't be long until racists are jailed merely for believing in white supremacy. Bigots may be contemptible and infuriating, but they are not criminals—at least not until they act on their intolerance. And when bigots do commit a crime, the punishment must be for the act itself—not for the thought that might have led to the act. A criminal's motivation for committing a crime, whether it is prejudice, peer pressure, greed, boredom, or any other reason, is irrelevant.

Political Correctness

Furthermore, if a criminal receives a more severe punishment because his or her beliefs are politically incorrect, then criminals whose crimes are politically correct receive a lesser punishment. Jeff Jacoby, a syndicated columnist, explains it this way: "A law that cracks down harder on criminals who harm members of certain groups by definition goes easier on those who target victims from other groups."[2] Robert Tracinski, editor of the *Intellectual Activist*, questions the disparity between the sentences for a bigot and the Unabomber, who sent mail bombs to college professors and businessmen:

> Why, for example, should a racist be prosecuted for the special crime of targeting blacks, while the Unabomber is not subject to special prosecution for his hatred of scientists and businessmen? The only

answer is that the Unabomber's environmentalist philosophy is considered more "politically correct" than the bigot's racism.[3]

By concentrating on the criminal's beliefs, the courts avoid focusing on the victims' rights, which should be the true aim of any judicial system. Tracinski notes, "Crimes can be whitewashed if done for the 'correct' political motives, while extra punishment can be meted out to those with 'incorrect' motives."[4]

The Fourteenth Amendment

The underlying theme in all arguments against hate crime laws is laid out in the Fourteenth Amendment—the Constitution's guarantee of equality for all under the law. Hate crime laws flout this basic idea by giving minorities special protection, a concept that goes against the beliefs of the Founding Fathers. As syndicated columnist John Leo eloquently writes, "If all skulls are equally valuable, as the first line of the Declaration of Independence says they are, then why don't all skull crackings deserve similar sentences?"[5] In effect, hate crime laws make some people more equal than others, dividing both victims and assailants into two classes.

The first class includes those associated with hate crimes. By imposing enhanced sentences on those convicted of hate crimes, society is arguing that hate crimes are a more serious crime than "ordinary" crimes and that victims of hate crimes suffer more than "regular" victims. Therefore, the logic goes, hate crime thugs need to suffer more for their sins. In the second class are the victims and criminals in non–hate crime cases. Don Feder, author and syndicated columnist, explains how "regular" crime victims interpret hate crime laws:

> "Since what happened to you (your assault, your rape, your murder) isn't quite as important, because it wasn't incited by malice against a protected class, we won't punish it as harshly." It is nothing less than a slap in the face to the vast majority of victims.[6]

The family of a black man who is murdered for $20 feels just as much pain over his death as the family of a black man who is killed by a violent racist. The "ordinary" murder is no less awful because it is not a hate crime. Regardless of the motive for the crime, Feder asserts that all crimes share the same roots:

> Crime is synonymous with hatred. Murders aren't committed out of love for the victim. Rapists aren't guided by a deep-seated affection. Assault with a deadly weapon isn't an expression of respect and admiration. Malice and envy lie at the heart of almost every crime. Why single out one type of malevolence, one particular brand of animosity, for an extra measure of punishment?[7]

Because all crimes are rooted in hatred, it is wrong, illogical, and unconstitutional to punish those that are characterized as "hate crimes" more heavily than others. What is needed is to punish similar crimes in a comparable and equitable manner.

A Slippery Slope

We're standing on the downside of a slippery slope right now. Hate crime laws—while noble in theory—conflict with Americans' rights to free speech and equality under the law. If hate crime laws are allowed to stand and proliferate, they will inevitably lead to the outlawing of offensive speech and thought. What is also inevitable is that critics of hate speech and hate crimes will continue to push for the criminalization of ideas, actions, and policies that are even slightly critical of politically correct ideas. The only way for society to ensure that speech will remain free is to allow *all* speech to remain free. The Constitution guarantees it.

1. *New Republic*, "The Hate Debate," November 2, 1998, p. 7.

2. Jeff Jacoby, "Hate Crimes Send the Wrong Message," *Boston Globe*, June 22, 2000, p. A25.

3. Robert Tracinski, "Politicizing Hate Crime," *Intellectual Activist*, April 1999, p. 2.

4. Tracinski, "Politicizing Hate Crime."

5. John Leo, "Punishing Hate Crimes," *U.S. News & World Report*, October 26, 1998, p. 20.

6. Don Feder, "Q: Are Hate-Crime Laws in Keeping with a Free Society? No: These Laws Assault Our First Amendment Rights and Will Lead to Thought Control," *Insight*, September 20, 1999, p. 41.

7. Feder, "Q: Are Hate-Crime Laws in Keeping with a Free Society? No: These Laws Assault Our First Amendment Rights," p. 42.

STUDY QUESTIONS

Chapter 1

1. According to Viewpoint 1, what factors are responsible for the growth of the racist organization National Alliance? What role has the Internet played in the development of hate groups? Should the government ban hate groups from hosting hate sites? Why or why not?

2. What is a "lone wolf"? According to Viewpoint 2, what are three reasons why lone wolves are more dangerous than hate groups? According to Viewpoint 3, what percentage of hate crimes are committed by lone wolves?

3. Viewpoint 4 contends that hate groups cannot be held responsible for crimes committed by their members. How does Viewpoint 3 respond to this argument? Do you believe that hate groups and their leaders should be charged as well with criminal behavior when their members commit hate crimes? Explain your answer.

4. According to Viewpoint 4, what rationale do white supremacist groups use to support their quest for a white homeland, free of minority and Jewish influence? Do you think separate homelands for different races or religions is achievable? Is it desirable? Why or why not? The state of Israel was carved out of Palestine and given to the Jews so they could have their own homeland. Is the Jewish State of Israel different from an Aryan nation? Why or why not?

Chapter 2

1. According to Viewpoint 2, "no hate speech means no free speech." Do you agree with this statement? Why or why not? Support your answer with examples from the viewpoints.

2. Many schools instituted speech codes because they believed minority students' ability to learn would be hindered if they were subjected to racial slurs and epithets. According to Viewpoint 2, however, the policy often backfired, with more minorities prosecuted under the speech code than whites. Based on the viewpoints, do you think speech codes are helpful or harmful? Explain.

3. Organizations that monitor hate groups are alarmed by hate groups' use of the Internet to recruit new members and spread racist propaganda. According to Viewpoint 3, hate content on the Internet is a serious problem that must be restricted. Do you agree? Why or why not?

4. Viewpoint 3 argues that parents can protect their children from hate and racism on the Internet by using filters—either from the Internet service provider or specially designed software. How does Viewpoint 4 respond to the argument for using filters? Do you think filters are an effective and practical response to hate on the Internet? Why or why not?

Chapter 3

1. Viewpoint 1 argues that hate crimes' damaging effects on society warrant punishing hate crimes more harshly than "ordinary" crimes, while Viewpoint 2 contends that murders committed as hate crimes are already severely punished. Is Viewpoint 2's argument valid for crimes that are less serious? For example, should painting graffiti consisting of swastikas or "KKK" on a synagogue be punished the same as painting graffiti promoting a high school class on a bridge? Why or why not?

2. Viewpoint 2 contends that hate crime laws will lead to thought control by first restricting hate speech and eventually restricting and censoring other types of speech. Based on your readings of the viewpoints in this book, do you agree with this argument? Explain your answer.

3. Viewpoint 3 claims that hate crime laws are necessary to afford all citizens equal protection under the law. How does Viewpoint 4 respond to this contention? Which argument is stronger? Why?

4. According to Viewpoint 4, a criminal's motive and intent when committing a crime is irrelevant and should not be punished by hate crime laws. Viewpoint 3 contends, however, that motive and intent are relevant to the charge and the severity of the sentence. Based on your reading of the viewpoints, should a criminal's beliefs, thoughts, or speech be considered when he or she is charged with or sentenced for a hate crime? Explain your answer.

Appendix A: Facts About Hate Groups

Hate Groups

- The number of active hate groups in the United States fell to 457 in 1999 from 537 in 1998, according to the Southern Poverty Law Center (SPLC), a hate-monitoring group.
- The first hate site on the Internet, known as Stormfront, was established in 1995 by a former Klansman named Don Black. As of early 2000, the SPLC estimates there are now 305 hate sites on the Internet, up from 254 in 1999; while the Simon Wiesenthal Center, which includes sites originating outside the United States, puts the number at 2,800.
- Hate groups sell 50,000 CDs of racist music over the Internet annually, according to the SPLC.
- According to the Anti-Defamation League, the white supremacist group National Alliance (NA) is the single most dangerous organized hate group in the United States. It maintains that the NA is the largest and most active neo-Nazi group, with about 1,000 members in 16 chapters in 26 states. William Pierce, author of *The Turner Diaries*, an explicit terrorism manual, is the leader of the NA.

Hate Crimes and Victims

- The number of hate crimes committed each year steadily declined in the latter half of the 1990s. According to the FBI, there were 8,759 hate crimes in 1996, 8,049 in 1997, and 7,755 in 1998, the last year for which figures are available.
- The targets of 80 percent of all hate crime are individuals: the remaining 20 percent include businesses, religious organizations, and various other targets.
- The FBI reports that a total of 33 people were murdered in 1996, 1997, and 1998 during incidents motivated by hate.
- About 66 percent of hate crimes are committed by "thrill seekers," often youths looking for excitement by attacking someone who is different.
- Thirty-three percent of hate crimes are considered "defensive," as whites strike out against minorities who have moved into previously all-white schools or neighborhoods.
- Less than 1 percent of hate crimes are committed by "true

believers," members of organized hate groups who believe they have a "mission" to eliminate their "enemies."

- Forty-one states and the District of Columbia have hate crime laws that include race, religion, ethnicity, and in some cases, disability and gender as protected categories. Of those 41 states, 21 include sexual orientation as a protected category.

- Nine states have no hate crime laws.

Notorious Hate Crimes

- On November 13, 1988, in Portland, Oregon, Mulugeta Seraw, an Ethiopian immigrant, was murdered by skinheads Kenneth Mieske, Steven Strasser, and Kyle Brewster. Acting on behalf of Seraw's family, Morris Dees of the Southern Poverty Law Center sued Tom Metzger and his son John, leaders of the White Aryan Resistance, for civil damages on the grounds that they encouraged and instigated the skinheads' crime. The Metzgers were found liable in 1990 for Seraw's murder and ordered to pay a total of $12.5 million.

- On June 7, 1998, three white men in a pickup truck chained James Byrd Jr., a black man, by his feet to the truck's back bumper and dragged him along an asphalt road for nearly two miles. John William King, an ex-con with ties to the white supremacist group Aryan Nation; Russell Brewer; and Shawn Berry were all convicted of Byrd's murder. King and Brewer were sentenced to death; Berry was given a life sentence.

- On October 6, 1998, Matthew Shepard, a gay college student in Laramie, Wyoming, met two men in a bar who lured him outside and severely beat him, tied him to a fence, and left him for dead. Passers-by, who thought he was a scarecrow, discovered the comatose Shepard the next day. He died October 12. Russell Henderson and Aaron McKinney are serving life sentences for his murder.

- Benjamin Smith, a member of the white supremacist organization World Church of the Creator, shot and killed two minorities and wounded nine others during a three-day killing spree in Indiana and Illinois in July 1999. Smith shot himself after a police chase as he was about to be apprehended by police.

- Buford O. Furrow, a white supremacist and member of the neo-Nazi group Aryan Nations, entered the Jewish Community Center in Granada Hills outside of Los Angeles in August 1999, where he shot and wounded five people, four of them children. After he left the center, he fatally shot Joseph Ileto, a Filipino-American mail carrier.

Hate Groups on Trial

- In 1981 Michael Donald was on his way to a store in Mobile, Alabama, when two members of the United Klans of America abducted and lynched him. His murderers were arrested and convicted. The Southern Poverty Law Center believed a conspiracy was behind the lynching, and in 1987 it filed a civil suit against the UKA. A $7 million judgment against the United Klans of America and its Klan members forced the hate group to turn over the deed to its headquarters to Donald's mother, Beulah Mae Donald. In addition, the FBI reopened the case and two other Klan members were convicted of criminal charges in Donald's murder. The UKA was responsible for much racial violence during the 1960s; Klan members assaulted Freedom Riders, murdered Viola Liuzzo during the Selma-Montgomery march, and bombed the 16th Street Baptist Church in Birmingham, killing four black girls.

- After a group of civil rights marchers were attacked in Georgia in 1987 by members of the Invisible Empire, Knights of the Ku Klux Klan, the Southern Poverty Law Center filed civil suit on their behalf. The Invisible Empire KKK is the nation's largest and most violent Klan group. The 1988 verdict against the Klan forced it to disband, destroy its membership lists, donate all its assets to the National Association for the Advancement of Colored People, and pay $37,500 to the marchers.

- During a rash of arsons against black churches in the South, the Macedonia Baptist Church in South Carolina was burned in 1995. The Southern Poverty Law Center brought suit against the Christian Knights of the Ku Klux Klan, based in North Carolina, and the Klan's North Carolina leader, Horace King. In 1998 a jury awarded the church $37.8 million in the largest judgment against a hate group to date—$15 million from the national Christian Knights KKK, $15 million from King, and $7 million from the South Carolina chapter. In addition, three Klansmen were assessed punitive damages of $100,000 and a fourth was ordered to pay $200,000.

- In 1998, Victoria Keenan and her son Jason stopped their car in front of the Aryan Nations compound in Hayden Lake, Idaho, to retrieve some papers that blew out of their car. Driving off, their car reportedly backfired, which the Aryan Nations guards mistook for gunfire. The guards jumped in their pickup truck and followed the Keenans. The Keenans' car was forced into a ditch after being fired on by the guards. The guards then beat both Victoria Keenan and Jason Keenan. The three guards were convicted of aggravated assault. The Southern Poverty Law Center filed a civil suit against Aryan Nations and its leader, Richard Butler. A jury awarded the Keenans $6.3 million in compensatory and punitive damages in September 2000 from the Aryan Nations, Butler, and the guards involved.

Famous Trials Concerning the Right of Free Speech

- *R.A.V. v. St. Paul* (1992): Shortly after a black family moved into an all-white neighborhood in St. Paul, Minnesota, a group of young men erected a burning cross in their front yard. They were arrested and convicted of violating a St. Paul ordinance that prohibited the public display of "a symbol, object, appellation, characterization or graffiti" that "arouses anger, alarm, or resentment in others on the basis of race, color, creed, religion, or gender." One defendant, Robert A. Viktora, appealed his conviction on the grounds that it violated his right to free speech. Ultimately, the U.S. Supreme Court struck down the St. Paul ordinance, ruling that it discriminated against particular forms of speech.

- *Wisconsin v. Mitchell* (1993): Todd Mitchell, a black nineteen-year-old, urged friends to beat up a young white boy. Although Mitchell himself did not participate in the beating, he was convicted of felony aggravated battery and given an additional sentence because his crime was motivated by hate. Mitchell appealed, claiming the extra punishment violated his right to free speech. The U.S. Supreme Court upheld his sentence, ruling that the penalty enhancement punished Mitchell's conduct, not his speech.

APPENDIX B: RELATED DOCUMENTS

Document 1: The First Amendment

The First Amendment to the U.S. Constitution is part of the Bill of Rights. It was ratified by the states on December 15, 1791. The Supreme Court has ruled that the amendment protects offensive speech, but not speech that incites violence.

Amendment I

Congress shall make no law respecting an establishment of religion, or prohibiting the free exercise thereof; or abridging the freedom of speech, or of the press; or the right of the people peaceably to assemble, and to petition the Government for a redress of grievances.

Document 2: The Fourteenth Amendment

The Fourteenth Amendment was added after the Civil War to protect the rights of freed black slaves in the South. Despite the fact that every former Confederate state except Tennessee had refused to ratify the amendment, it became law in July 1868.

Section 1.

All persons born or naturalized in the United States, and subject to the jurisdiction thereof, are citizens of the United States and of the State wherein they reside. No State shall make or enforce any law which shall abridge the privileges or immunities of citizens of the United States; nor shall any State deprive any person of life, liberty, or property, without due process of law; nor deny to any person within its jurisdiction the equal protection of the laws.

Document 3: The Hate Crimes Prevention Act of 1999

President Bill Clinton had urged Congress to pass the Hate Crimes Prevention Act since 1997. The act would add the categories of gender, sexual orientation, and disability to other protected classes. As of October 2000, he had been unable to persuade Congress to pass this legislation, parts of which are excerpted below.

Section 1. Short Title.

This Act may be cited as the 'Hate Crimes Prevention Act of 1999.'

Sec. 2. Findings.

Congress finds that—

(1) the incidence of violence motivated by the actual or perceived race, color, national origin, religion, sexual orientation, gender, or disability of the victim poses a serious national problem;

(2) such violence disrupts the tranquility and safety of communities and is deeply divisive;

(3) existing Federal law is inadequate to address this problem;

(4) such violence affects interstate commerce in many ways, including—

(A) by impeding the movement of members of targeted groups and forcing such members to move across State lines to escape the incidence or risk of such violence; and

(B) by preventing members of targeted groups from purchasing goods and services, obtaining or sustaining employment or participating in other commercial activity;

(5) perpetrators cross State lines to commit such violence;

(6) instrumentalities of interstate commerce are used to facilitate the commission of such violence;

(7) such violence is commited using articles that have traveled in interstate commerce;

(8) violence motivated by bias that is a relic of slavery can constitute badges and incidents of slavery;

(9) although many State and local authorities are now and will continue to be responsible for prosecuting the overwhelming majority of violent crimes in the United States, including violent crimes motivated by bias, Federal jurisdiction over certain violent crimes motivated by bias is necessary to supplement State and local jurisdiction and ensure that justice is achieved in each case;

(10) Federal jurisdiction over certain violent crimes motivated by bias enables Federal, State, and local authorities to work together as partners in the investigation and prosecution of such crimes; and

(11) the problem of hate crime is sufficiently serious, widespread, and interstate in nature as to warrant Federal assistance to States and local jurisdictions. . . .

Sec. 4. Prohibition of Certain Acts of Violence

. . . (c)(1) Whoever, whether or not acting under color of law, willfully causes bodily injury to any person or, through the use of fire, a firearm, or an explosive device, attempts to cause bodily injury to any person, because of the actual or perceived race, color, religion, or national origin of any person—

(A) shall be imprisoned not more than 10 years, or fined in accordance with this title, or both; and

(B) shall be imprisoned for any term of years or for life, or fined in accordance with this title, or both if—

(i) death results from the acts committed in violation of this paragraph; or

(ii) the acts committed in violation of this paragraph include kidnapping or an attempt to kidnap, aggravated sexual abuse or an attempt to commit aggravated sexual abuse, or an attempt to kill.

(2)(A) Whoever, whether or not acting under color of law, in any circumstance described in subparagraph (B), willfully causes bodily injury to any person or, through the use of fire, a firearm, or an explosive device, attempts to cause bodily injury to any person, because of the actual or perceived religion, gender, sexual orientation, or disability of any person—

(i) shall be imprisoned not more than 10 years, or fined in accordance with this title, or both; and

(ii) shall be imprisoned for any term of years or for life, or fined in accordance with this title, or both, if—

(I) death results from the acts committed in violation of this paragraph; or

(II) the acts committed in violation of this paragraph include kidnapping or an attempt to kidnap, aggravated sexual abuse or an attempt to commit aggravated sexual abuse, or an attempt to kill.

Document 4: Federal Legislation to Protect U.S. Citizens from the Ku Klux Klan

In response to terrorist activities against freed black slaves by the Ku Klux Klan in the South after the Civil War, Congress passed the Ku Klux Klan Act. The act set the fine and punishment for crimes committed to prevent any citizen from exercising his constitutionally protected rights, such as voting. It also made it illegal to prosecute or punish anyone because of his race or color.

18 U.S.C.

241. CONSPIRACY AGAINST RIGHTS OF CITIZENS

If two or more persons conspire to injure, oppress, threaten, or intimidate any citizen in the free exercise or enjoyment of any right or privilege secured to him by the Constitution or laws of the United States, or because of his having so exercised the same; or

If two or more persons go in disguise on the highway, or on the premises of another, with intent to prevent or hinder his free exercise or enjoyment of any right or privilege so secured

—They shall be fined not more than $10,000 or imprisoned not more than ten years, or both; and if death results, they shall be subject to imprisonment for any term of years or for life.

As amended Apr. 11, 1968, Pub.L. 90-284, Title I, 103(a), 82 Stat. 75.

242. DEPRIVATION OF RIGHTS UNDER COLOR OF LAW

Whoever, under color of any law, statute, ordinance, regulation, or custom, willfully subjects any inhabitant of any State, Territory, or District to the deprivation of any rights, privileges, or immunities secured or protected by the Constitution or laws of the United States, or to different punishments, pains, or penalties, on account of such inhabitant being an alien, or by reason of his color, or race, than are prescribed for the punishment of citizens, shall be fined not more than $1,000 or imprisoned not more than one year, or both; and if death results shall be subject to imprisonment for any term of years or for life.

Quoted in Wyn Craig Wade, *The Fiery Cross: The Ku Klux Klan in America.* New York: Oxford University Press, 1987.

Document 5: The Imperial Proclamation

The Ku Klux Klan began its second era of influence after the debut of the contro-versial film Birth of a Nation *in 1915. The movie portrayed the fortunes of a small southern town before, during, and after the Civil War, and depicted Klan members as courageous men who restored law and order in a time of chaos. William Simmons saw the film and was moved to revive the Ku Klux Klan. This excerpt is from his open invitation of July 4, 1916, to all white men to join the new Ku Klux Klan.*

We, the members of this order, desiring to promote real patriotism toward our civil Government; honorable peace among men and nations; protection for and happiness in the homes of our people; love, real brotherhood, mirth, and manhood among ourselves, and liberty, justice, and fraternity among all mankind; and believing we can best accomplish these noble pur-poses through the channel of a high-class mystic, social, patriotic, benevo-lent association, having a perfected lodge system with an exalted, ritualistic form of work and an effective form of government, not for selfish profit but for the mutual betterment, benefit, and protection of all our oath-bound associates, their welfare, physically, socially, morally, and vocationally, and their loved ones, do proclaim to the whole world that we are dedicated to the sublime and pleasant duty of providing generous aid, tender sympathy, and fraternal assistance in the effulgence of the light of life and amid the sable shadows of death, amid fortune and misfortune, and to the exalted privilege of demonstrating the practical utility of the great, yet most-neglected, doctrine of the fatherhood of God and the brotherhood of man as a vital force in the lives and affairs of men.

In this we invite all men who can qualify to become citizens of the invis-ible empire to approach the portal of our beneficent domain and join us in our noble work of extending its boundaries; in disseminating the gospel of "klankraft," thereby encouraging, conserving, protecting, and making vital the fraternal human relationship in the practice of a wholesome clanish-ness; to share with us the glory of performing the secred [sic] duty of pro-tecting womanhood; to maintain forever white supremacy in all things; to commemorate the holy and chivalric achievements of our fathers; to safe-guard the sacred rights, exalted privileges, and distinctive institutions of our civil Government; to bless mankind, and to keep eternally ablaze the secred [sic] fire of a fervent devotion to a pure Americanism.

The invisible empire is founded on sterling character and immutable principles based upon a most sacred sentiment and cemented by noble purposes; it is promoted by a sincere, unselfish devotion of the souls of manly men, and is managed and governed by the consecrated intelligence of thoughtful brains. It is the soul of chivalry and virtue's impenetrable shield—the devoute impulse of an unconquered race.

Quoted in Wyn Craig Wade, *The Fiery Cross: The Ku Klux Klan in America.* New York: Oxford University Press, 1987.

Document 6: The Ku Klux Klan Kreed

When William Simmons reestablished the Ku Klux Klan at the end of 1915, he incorporated many elements of the original Klan of the Civil War era. The following is an excerpt of the Ku Klux Klan Kreed, as revised by Brad Thompson, a former Grand Dragon of the American Knights of the Ku Klux Klan in Indiana during the mid-1990s, which gives the basic tenets of the KKK.

We, the Order of the Knights of the Ku Klux Klan, reverentially acknowledge the majesty and supremacy of the Divine Being, and recognize the goodness and providence of the same.

We recognize our relation to the government of the United States of America, the supremacy of its constitution, the union of the states thereunder, and the constitution and laws thereof, and shall be devoted to the sublime principles of a pure Americanism and valiant in the defense of its ideals and its institutions.

We avow the distinction between the races of mankind, as same has been by the Creator, and we shall ever be true in the faithful maintenance of white separatism and will strenuously oppose any compromise thereof in any and all things.

We appreciate the intrinsic value of a real practical fraternal relationship among men and women of kindred thought, purpose and ideals and the infinite benefits accruable therefrom, and we shall faithfully devote ourselves to the practice of an honorable klanishness that the life and living of each may be a constant blessing to others.

Quoted in Worth H. Weller and Brad Thompson, *Under the Hood: Unmasking the Modern Ku Klux Klan.* North Manchester, IN: DeWitt Books, 1998.

Document 7: What Is Creativity All About?

The World Church of the Creator was founded by Ben Klassen in 1973 and is now led by Matthew Hale. The church promotes a religion it calls Creativity. The following excerpt summarizes some of the beliefs of this white supremacist group.

After six thousand years of recorded history, our people finally have a religion of, for, and by them. CREATIVITY is that religion. It is established for the Survival, Expansion, and Advancement of our White Race exclusively. Indeed, we believe that what is good for the White Race is the highest virtue, and what is bad for the White Race is the ultimate sin.

We have come to hold these views by observing the Eternal Laws of Nature, by studying History, and by using the Logic and Common Sense everyone is born with: the highest Law of Nature is the survival of one's own kind; history has shown us that the White Race is responsible for all that which we call progress on this earth; and that it is therefore logical and sensible to place supreme importance upon Race and to reject all ideas which fail to do so.

Our people have faced threats throughout history, but never before has our people faced as grave a threat as it is facing today. Today, our people's very continued biological existence on this planet is in doubt. In 1920, for example, one out of every three people on this planet were White. Today, only one out of twelve are White. If present trends continue, one can only imagine what the complexion of the world will be like in another one hundred years.

How did this calamity come about? It came about because of our people's skewed thinking. Our people have thus far been concerned with every issue besides the issue of their own survival. We have subsidized those not of our own kind at our expense, causing their numbers to soar, while at the same time, White people have scaled back the size of their families, either out of selfishness or because of low-paying salaries and exorbitant taxes. We have divided ourselves into all kinds of organizations and causes, none of whom address the most basic issue: Will White children have a future? With CREATIVITY, this is the issue, and all other issues revolve around it.

Our people everywhere are beginning to embrace the dynamic and inspiring creed and program of CREATIVITY. White people everywhere are beginning to put aside their past differences and divisions and are coming together as one people for their best interests. More and more of our people are beginning to realize that if White people do not look out for their own future, no other people will. As a result, our churches are sprouting up all over the world, our ministers preaching the word of White unity and our members zealously spreading the word to you, our fellow White people. We hope that after reading this pamphlet, you will decide to obtain more information, will consequently decide to become a member of our church, The World Church of the Creator, and will decide to join us in this historic struggle.

Reprinted from "What Is Creativity All About?" by Matt Hale, by permission of the World Church of the Creator, PO Box 2002, East Peoria, IL 61611; www.creator.org.

ORGANIZATIONS TO CONTACT

The editors have compiled the following list of organizations concerned with the issues debated in this book. The descriptions are derived from materials provided by the organizations. All have publications or information available for interested readers. The list was compiled on the date of publication of the present volume; the information provided here may change. Be aware that many organizations take several weeks or longer to respond to inquiries, so allow as much time as possible.

Anti-Defamation League (ADL)
823 United Nations Plaza, New York, NY 10017
(212) 490-2525
website: www.adl.org

The ADL works to stop the defamation of Jews and to ensure fair treatment for all U.S. citizens. It advocates state and federal penalty enhancement laws to fight hate crimes. It publishes the quarterly *Facts* magazine and distributes reports such as *Hate Crimes Laws: A Comprehensive Guide*.

Aryan Nations
Church of Jesus Christ Christian
PO Box 362, Hayden Lake, ID 83835
e-mail: aryannhq@nidlink.com • website: www.nidlink.com/~aryanvic

Aryan Nations promotes racial purity and believes that whites are persecuted by Jews and blacks. It publishes the *Aryan Nations Newsletter* and pamphlets such as *New World Order in North America*, *Aryan Warriors Stand*, and *Know Your Enemies*.

HateWatch
PO Box 380151, Cambridge, MA 02238-0151
(617) 876-3796
e-mail: info@hatewatch.org • website: www.hatewatch.org

HateWatch is a Web-based organization that monitors hate group activity on the Internet. Its website features information on hate groups and civil rights organizations and their activities.

National Alliance
PO Box 90, Hillsboro, WV 24946
(304) 653-4600
website: www.natvan.com

The alliance believes that the white race is superior to all other races in intelligence, ability, and creativity. It argues that it is the obligation of all whites to fight for the creation of a white nation that is free of non-Aryan influence. It publishes the newsletter *Free Speech* and the magazine *National Vanguard*.

National Association for the Advancement of Colored People (NAACP)
4805 Mt. Hope Dr., Baltimore, MD 21215-3297
(410) 358-8900 • fax: (410) 486-9255
information hot line: (410) 521-4939
website: www.naacp.org

The NAACP is the oldest and largest civil rights organization in the United States. Its principal objective is to ensure the political, educational, social, and economic equality of minorities. It publishes the magazine *Crisis* ten times a year as well as a variety of newsletters, books, and pamphlets.

National Gay and Lesbian Task Force (NGLTF)
2320 17th St. NW, Washington, DC 20009-2702
(202) 332-6483 • fax: (202) 332-0207
e-mail: ngltf@ngltf.org • website: www.ngltf.org

NGLTF is a civil rights organization that fights bigotry and violence against gays and lesbians. It sponsors conferences and organizes local groups to promote civil rights legislation for gays and lesbians. It publishes the monthly *Eye on Equality* column and distributes reports, fact sheets, and bibliographies on antigay violence.

Southern Poverty Law Center/Klanwatch Project
PO Box 2087, Montgomery, AL 36102
(205) 264-0286
website: www.splcenter.org

The center litigates civil cases to protect the rights of poor people, particularly when those rights are threatened by white supremacist groups. The affiliated Klanwatch Project and the Militia Task Force collect data on white supremacist groups and militias. The center publishes numerous books and reports as well as the monthly *Klanwatch Intelligence Report*.

Stormfront
PO Box 6637, West Palm Beach, FL 33405
(561) 833-0030 • fax: (561) 820-0051
e-mail: comments@stormfront.org • website: www.stormfront.org

Stormfront is dedicated to preserving "white western culture, ideals, and freedom of speech." It serves as a resource for white political and social action groups. It publishes the weekly newsletter *Stormwatch*, and its website contains articles and position papers such as *White Nationalism: Key Concepts* and *Equality: Man's Most Dangerous Myth*.

White Aryan Resistance (WAR)
PO Box 65, Fallbrook, CA 92088
(760) 723-8996 • hotline: (800) 923-1813
e-mail: warmetzger@funtv.com • website: www.resist.com

WAR believes the white race is in danger of extinction and advocates the establishment of a separatist state for whites only. It publishes the monthly newspaper *WAR*, produces the *Race and Reason* television show, distributes "white power" music recordings, and maintains a racialist news and information hotline.

World Church of the Creator (WCOTC)
P.O. Box 2002, East Peoria, IL 61611
(309) 699-0135 • hotline: (309) 699-0135
e-mail: PMHale1@aol.com • website: www.creator.org

WCOTC is a religion that is based on love for the white race above all others. Its goal is to ensure the expansion and advancement of the white race, and its members believe that nature's highest law requires each species to fight for its own survival. It publishes *Nature's Eternal Religion, The White Man's Bible*, and the monthly *The Struggle*.

FOR FURTHER READING

Richard Abanes, *American Militias: Rebellion, Racism, and Religion*. Downers Grove, IL: InterVarsity Press, 1996. Abanes explains where paramilitary groups come from, who their members are, what their beliefs are, and how they are organized and motivated. He describes many of the complex conspiracy theories that have gained a following among militia members, shows how racism and religion fuel many of their bizarre beliefs and goals, and suggests how their sometimes dangerous zealotry might be defused.

Vincent Coppola, *Dragons of God: A Journey Through Far-Right America*. Atlanta: Longstreet Press, 1996. Coppola exposes the far-right network of Christian Identity, Aryan Nations, skinheads, Ku Klux Klan, and other radicals and religious fanatics in contemporary America. He concludes that much of their discontent can be blamed on poor economic opportunities.

Jack Levin and Jack McDevitt, *Hate Crimes: The Rising Tide of Bigotry and Bloodshed*. New York: Plenum Press, 1993. The authors present a detailed examination of the increasing phenomenon of hate crimes, explain how these crimes affect their victims, and suggest how society should respond to hate crimes.

Nancy MacLean, *Behind the Mask of Chivalry: The Making of the Second Ku Klux Klan*. New York: Oxford University Press, 1994. MacLean presents the inner workings of the Ku Klux Klan, how it achieved its level of power and influence, and why millions of followers were convinced to join this secretive organization.

David A. Neiwert, *In God's Country: The Patriot Movement and the Pacific Northwest*. Pullman: Washington State University Press, 1999. The Pacific Northwest is home to the white supremacist groups Christian Identity and Phineas Priest, as well as many militia groups, survivalists, and others who believe the government is conspiring to take away constitutionally protected freedoms. Neiwert examines this phenomenon through interviews, historical research, and first-person accounts.

James Ridgeway, *Blood in the Face: The Ku Klux Klan, Aryan Nations, Nazi Skinheads, and the Rise of a New White Culture*. 2nd ed. New York: Thunder's Mouth Press, 1995. In this in-depth study, the author traces the rise of the white supremacist movement and militias, their tactics, and their impact. Ridgeway uses interviews, photos, police reports, and recruiting pamphlets to tell the story of armed, white hate groups.

Patsy Sims, *The Klan*. 2nd ed. Lexington: University Press of Kentucky, 1996. Through personal interviews and firsthand experiences, Sims provides a detailed look at some of the Ku Klux Klan's leaders and the victims of their intimidation and terrorism.

Worth H. Weller and Brad Thompson, *Under the Hood: Unmasking the Modern Ku Klux Klan*. North Manchester, IN: DeWitt Books, 1998. Thompson, a former Grand Dragon with the American Knights of the Ku Klux Klan in Indiana, explains what led him to join this organization, how he rose through the ranks in three years to become its leader, and why, after three years in the Klan, he became disillusioned and quit.

WORKS CONSULTED

Books

Donald Altschiller, *Hate Crimes: A Reference Handbook.* Santa Barbara, CA: ABC-CLIO, 1999. An excellent resource about hate crime. It contains a basic overview of hate crime and legislation to combat it, a chronology, biographical sketches of people involved in fighting hate crime, statistics and documents from government agencies and other organizations, a list of organizations, and a bibliography.

Howard L. Bushart, John R. Craig, and Myra Barnes, *Soldiers of God: White Supremacists and Their Holy War for America.* New York: Kensington Books, 1998. The authors examine white supremacist groups such as Aryan Nations, Christian Identity, skinheads, and the Ku Klux Klan from the perspective of the members themselves. The groups' leaders explain in interviews their beliefs and views on racial identity, religion, race relations, welfare, and immigration.

David M. Chalmers, *Hooded Americanism: The History of the Ku Klux Klan.* Durham, NC: Duke University Press, 1998. Chalmers chronicles the history of the Ku Klux Klan from its beginnings after the Civil War to the late 1970s. He discusses its strongest period in the 1920s and the turbulence of the 1960s and how the Klan inadvertently helped bring about the civil rights legislation it opposed so strongly.

Betty A. Dobratz and Stephanie L. Shanks-Meile, *"White Power, White Pride!" The White Separatist Movement in the United States.* New York: Twayne, 1997. The authors examine the history, ideology, and strategies of the white separatist movement—specifically the Ku Klux Klan, neo-Nazis, Christian Identity, and skinheads—through interviews with the groups' leaders and members, original documents, and firsthand observations at rallies and other meetings.

Paul Elliott, *Brotherhoods of Fear: A History of Violent Organizations.* New York: Sterling, 1998. Elliott traces the history of organizations that have inspired fear, terror, hatred, and paranoia over the centuries, including the Inquisition, Ku Klux Klan, Mafia, religious cults, and others.

Owen M. Fiss, *The Irony of Free Speech.* Cambridge, MA: Harvard University Press, 1996. Hate speech is just one of the issues of free speech discussed in this slim volume. Fiss argues that the government can protect and defend free speech by both restricting harmful speech *and* requiring opposing points of views to be heard.

Maureen Harrison and Steve Gilbert, eds., *Freedom of Speech Decisions of the United States Supreme Court.* San Diego: Excellent Books, 1996. This excellent reference book contains excerpts of the decisions in thirteen court cases that involve freedom of speech issues. Included are the decisions on "fighting words" in *Chaplinsky v. New Hampshire* and hate speech in *Brandenburg v. Ohio* and *R.A.V. v. St. Paul.*

Laura J. Lederer and Richard Delgado, eds., *The Price We Pay: The Case Against Racist Speech, Hate Propaganda, and Pornography.* New York: Hill and Wang, 1995. This collection of essays maintains that "the price we pay" for permitting hate speech and pornography is too high. The authors link hate speech and pornography with hate crimes and violence against women, and contend that the right of equality under the law should come before the right to free speech.

Catharine MacKinnon, *Only Words.* Cambridge, MA: Harvard University Press, 1993. MacKinnon argues that pornography and hate speech are not "only words," that they are, in fact, acts of intimidation, terrorism, and discrimination. MacKinnon maintains that the law should be concerned not with what the words say, but what they do.

Richard K. Tucker, *The Dragon and the Cross: The Rise and Fall of the Ku Klux Klan in Middle America.* Hamden, CT: Archon Books, 1991. Tucker discusses the leader of the Ku Klux Klan in Indiana in 1925 and the scandal that led to his imprisonment and the disgrace of the KKK.

Wyn Craig Wade, *The Fiery Cross: The Ku Klux Klan in America.* New York: Oxford University Press, 1987. Wade traces the Ku Klux Klan from its beginnings after the Civil War to the late 1980s. The appendices include original KKK documents.

Jonathan Wallace and Mark Mangan, *Sex, Laws, and Cyberspace: Freedom and Regulation on the Frontiers of the Online Revolution.* New York: Henry Holt, 1996. The authors discuss the ethical and legal issues involved in hate speech and pornography on the Internet. They defend the right to free speech in cyberspace and suggest ways that it can be monitored without violating the First Amendment.

Rita Kirk Whillock and David Slayden, eds., *Hate Speech.* Thousand Oaks, CA: Sage, 1995. Nine essays examine intolerance and hate speech in controversial issues ranging from gay rights and abortion to affirmative action. The authors discuss how hate speech and rage appear in the media, popular culture, and political rhetoric, among other forums.

Periodicals

Atlanta Constitution, "Targeting Hate Crimes," February 22, 1999.

———, "A Tool Against Terrorism," October 19, 1998.

Howard P. Berkowitz, "Q: Are Hate-Crime Laws in Keeping with a Free Society? Yes: Such Laws Send a Powerful Message to Racists and Bigots Everywhere," *Insight*, September 20, 1999.

Josiah H. Brown, "In Memory of Free Speech," *Wall Street Journal*, November 27, 1996.

Bill Dedman, "Midwest Gunman Had Engaged in Racist Acts at Two Universities," *New York Times*, July 6, 1999.

Sandi Dolbee, "To White Supremacist Metzger, Racist Crusade Is 'Nothing Personal,'" *San Diego Union-Tribune*, November 10, 1995.

Richard Dooling, "Punish Crime, Not Hate," *Wall Street Journal*, July 20, 1998.

Toby Eckert, "Hate Groups Find Web Useful Tool to Spread Word," *San Diego Union-Tribune*, November 9, 1999.

Susan Estrich, "The Threat Posed by Hate Groups," *Liberal Opinion Week*, August 23, 1999.

Don Feder, "Q: Are Hate-Crime Laws in Keeping with a Free Society? No: These Laws Assault Our First Amendment Rights and Will Lead to Thought Control," *Insight*, September 20, 1999.

Gary Greenebaum, "Racists Can Justify Anything, Even Child Murder," *Liberal Opinion Week*, August 23, 1999.

Tom Hayden, "These Aren't Isolated Acts of Violence," *Liberal Opinion Week*, August 23, 1999.

Jeff Jacoby, "Hate Crimes Send the Wrong Message," *Boston Globe*, June 22, 2000.

Edward M. Kennedy and Arlen Specter, "When Combating Hate Should Be a Federal Fight," *Washington Post*, December 1, 1997.

Brad Knickerbocker, "White Separatists Plot 'Pure' Society," *Christian Science Monitor*, April 20, 1995.

David Lehrer, "Tolerance, Not Hate, Is on the Rise," *Los Angeles Times*, August 13, 1999.

John Leo, "Punishing Hate Crimes," *U.S. News & World Report*, October 26, 1998.

Charles Levendosky, "One Man's Hate Speech, Another's Political Speech," *Liberal Opinion Week*, August 17, 1998.

Brian Levin, "Does America Need a Federal Hate-Crime Law? Yes: Hate Crimes Are Especially Threatening to Their Victims and to Our Pluralistic Democracy," *Insight*, November 23, 1998.

Jack Levin and Jack McDevitt, "The Research Needed to Understand Hate Crime," *Chronicle of Higher Education*, August 4, 1995.

Los Angeles Times, "Tackling the Haters," July 21, 1999.

Michael Marriott, "Rising Tide: Sites Born of Hate," *New York Times*, March 18, 1999.

Paul K. McMasters, "Must a Civil Society Be a Censored Society?" *Human Rights*, Fall 1999.

Frank Morriss, "Senate Vote on Hate Crimes Sweeps Aside Serious Considerations," *Wanderer*, August 5, 1999.

New Republic, "The Hate Debate," November 2, 1998.

New York Times, "Murdered for Who He Was," October 13, 1998.

Jennifer Oldham, "Wiesenthal Center Compiles List of Hate-Based Websites," *Los Angeles Times*, December 18, 1997.

Jared Sandberg, "Spinning a Web of Hate," *Newsweek*, July 19, 1999.

Gordon Smith and Ken Hallinan, "L.A. Shooting Suspect Held on Murder Charge," *San Diego Union-Tribune*, August 12, 1999.

Jo Thomas, "New Face of Terror Crimes: 'Lone Wolf' Weaned on Hate," *New York Times*, August 16, 1999.

Robert Tracinski, "Politicizing Hate Crime," *Intellectual Activist*, April 1999.

David Tyler, "Social Inequality Fosters Resentment and Frustration Hate Groups Feed On," *New Unionist*, February 2000.

Washington Post, "The Aryan Nations Verdict," September 16, 2000.

George Will, "Hate Crimes: An Extension of Identity Politics," *Conservative Chronicle*, October 21, 1998.

Eric Zorn, "Free Speech Is the Only Refuge of a Hatemonger," *Liberal Opinion Week*, July 19, 1999.

Internet Sources

Anti-Defamation League, "Explosion of Hate: The Growing Danger of the National Alliance," www.adl.org/Frames/front_explosion_ of_hate.html.

Center for New Community, "World Church of the Creator: One Year Later," June 26, 2000, www.newcomm.org/bdi/wcotc.pdf.

Bill Clinton, remarks by the president at the White House Conference on Hate Crimes, Washington, D.C., November 10, 1997, www.whitehouse.gov/uri-res/I2R?urn:pdi://oma.eop.gov.us/1997/11/12/1.text.1.

———, remarks by the president on Hate Crimes, April 25, 2000, www.pub.whitehouse.gov/uri-res/I2R?urn:pdi://oma.eop.gov.us/2000/4/26/8.text.1.

Ros Davidson, "Web of Hate," *Salon.com*, October 16, 1998, www.salon.com/news/1998/10/16newsa.html.

Roger Ebert, "When the Web Is in the Headline," *ZDNet*, October 1999, www.zdnet.com/yil/content/columnists/ebert9910.html.

David Hipschman, "Dealing with Hate on the Net," *WebReview*, November 10, 1995, http://webreview.com/nov10/features/hate/index.html.

Jay Hughes, "Racist Church Membership Increases," AP Online, July 2, 2000, wwws.elibrary.com.

Edward Kennedy, "Bill Summary of the Hate Crimes Prevention Act Amendment," June 19, 2000, www.senate.gov/~kennedy/statements/00/06/2000620E14.html.

———, "Statement of Senator Edward M. Kennedy: Hate Crimes Prevention Act Amendment," June 16, 2000, www.senate.gov/~kennedy/statements/00/06/2000620E04.html.

———, "Statement of Senator Edward M. Kennedy on the Hate Crimes Prevention Act Amendment to the DoD Authorization Bill," June 1, 2000, www.senate.gov/~kennedy/statements/00/06/2000620E12.html.

Ted Koppel, transcript, "Hate and the Internet," *Nightline*, January 13, 1997, www.stormfront.org/dblack/nightline011398.htm.

Mike McLean, "Aryans Lose," *Coeur d'Alene Press Online*, September 8, 2000, www.cdapress.com/archives/0908/news2.html.

———, "Edgar Steele Speaks Out," *Coeur d'Alene Press Online*, September 5, 2000, www.cdapress.com/archives/0905/news2.html.

———, "Judge Says Butler Can Be Held Liable for Guards' Assault," *Coeur d'Alene Press Online*, September 2, 2000, www.cdapress.com/archives/0902/news2.html.

————, "Litigation Pushing Racists Underground," *Coeur d'Alene Press Online*, September 6, 2000. www.cdapress.com/archives/0906/news2.html

Lisa Napoli, "Web of Hate," *MSNBC.com*, September 12, 1999, www.msnbc.com/news/458895.asp?0na=22076X0&cpl=1.

Pete Peters, "How Far Will They Go?" n.d., www.identity.org/index.html/how_far.html.

————, "The Label Identity," n.d., www.identity.org/index.html/the_label.html.

Janet Reno, "Attorney General Reno Delivers Statement on Hate Crimes," April 25, 2000, wwws.elibrary.com.

Scott Rosenberg, "The Web Can't Make Racists," *Salon.com*, July 9, 1999, www.salon.com/tech/col/rose/1999/07/09/.

Rick Savage, "Frequently Asked Questions About Creativity," n.d., www.creator.org/faq/html.

Southern Poverty Law Center, "Fewer, but Harder," www.splcenter.org/teachingtolerance/tt-index.html.

————, "The Year in Hate," *Intelligence Report*, Winter 2000, www.splcenter.org/intelligenceproject/ip-4m2.html.

Charles Weisman, "A Debate on Race and the Bible," n.d., www.seek-info.com/debate.htm.

Wisconsin v. Mitchell, (92-515), 508 U.S. 47 (1993), http://supct.law.cornell.edu/supct/html/92-515.ZO.html.

World Church of the Creator, "FAQ About Creativity," www.creator.org/faq.html.

Congressional Testimony

Abraham Cooper, testimony on "Hate on the Internet," before the Senate Committee on the Judiciary, September 14, 1999.

Eric H. Holder Jr., testimony before the Committee on the Judiciary, U.S. House of Representatives, Concerning Hate Crimes, August 4, 1999.

Joseph T. Roy, testimony before the U.S. Senate Committee on the Judiciary, "Hate on the Internet," September 14, 1999.

INDEX

ABOUT THE AUTHOR

Tamara Roleff is a freelance writer and former senior editor for Greenhaven Press. She has a degree in English from Iowa State University and worked as a newspaper reporter and editor before editing books for Greenhaven Press. She has lived and traveled all over the world, but San Diego will always be her home.